IT HAPPENED IN BOSTON

It Happened In Series

IT HAPPENED IN
BOSTON

Julia Boulton Clinger

TWODOT®

GUILFORD, CONNECTICUT
HELENA, MONTANA

AN IMPRINT OF THE GLOBE PEQUOT PRESS

A · **T W O D O T**® · **B O O K**

Copyright © 2007 Morris Book Publishing, LLC

Front cover photo: Busy street scene at Market Street and Court Street, ca. 1895. Library of Congress, LC-USZ62-96214
Back cover photo: Ruth, Shore, Foster, and Gainer of the Boston Red Sox. Library of Congress, LC-USZ62-23241
Text design by Nancy Freeborn
Map by M. A. Dubé © 2007 Morris Book Publishing, LLC

Library of Congress Cataloging-in-Publication Data
Clinger, Julia.
 It happened in Boston / Julia Clinger.—1st ed.
  p. cm.— (It happened in series)
 Includes bibliographical references and index.
 ISBN-13: 978-0-7627-4134-2
 ISBN-10: 0-7627-4134-1
 1. Boston (Mass.)—History—Anecdotes. 2. Boston (Mass.)—Biography—Anecdotes. I. Title.
 F73.36.C58 2007
 974.4'61—dc22

                                                              2006036212

Manufactured in the United States of America
First Edition/First Printing

For Boulton and Porter, Bostonians both

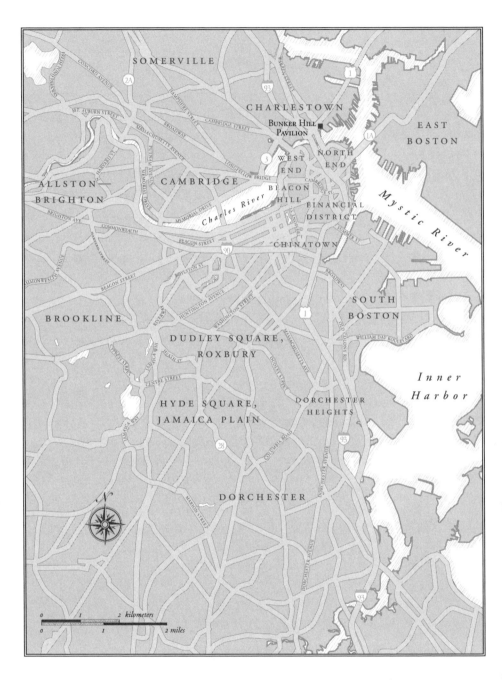

BOSTON

CONTENTS

CONTENTS

INTRODUCTION

Boston's timeline is rife with reversals and contradictions. Since its inception as a "city on the hill" founded by righteous Puritans, it has been a Brahmin stronghold and a multicultural melting pot, a cradle of liberty and a crucible of intolerance, the "Athens of America" and a breeding ground for backdoor politics. Even its topography is a study in opposites, spanning several neighborhoods (among them the South End and the Back Bay) created by landfills and an excavation (the Big Dig) that remains the largest public works project ever attempted in America.

Uniting these polarities is the civic theme of survival in the face of steep odds: from the beleaguered troop that held its own in the Battle of Bunker Hill to the self-described "idiots" that banished the eighty-six-year Curse of the Bambino, Boston's reputation is built on its ability to overcome adversity and emerge with its character intact. Just as the city has preserved its history without becoming a museum (an accomplishment that is instantly perceptible on the Freedom Trail, where Revolutionary landmarks and soaring skyscrapers coexist in apparent harmony), it has managed to retain its essence despite upheavals including the Revolution, abolitionism, industrialization, immigration, the Depression, race riots, and scandals surrounding the Catholic Church.

This essence combines idealism and antagonism, innovation and tradition, inclusiveness and elitism. In keeping with its history, constituency, and landscape, Boston's character is an oxymoron of sorts, a living illustration of the adage that the more things change, the more they stay the same.

THE EXECUTION OF GOODY GLOVER

- 1688 -

THE CHILL WINDS OF NOVEMBER DIDN'T DETER THE CROWD surrounding the gallows on Boston Common, where they'd gathered to watch the execution of a proven witch. Goody Glover may have looked like a harmless old woman, but she'd been convicted of placing a curse on four Puritan children. In keeping with her supposed allegiance to the dark side, the crone showed no remorse even in the shadow of the hangman's noose. According to the Puritan minister who had worked tirelessly to establish her guilt, she faced death with a vow that her young victims would remain "in their furnace as before, and it [would grow] rather seven times hotter than it was."

Worse torments were unimaginable to those who had witnessed the children under Goody Glover's spell. Their symptoms would have tested the resources of even Mary Poppins: Within a matter of days in the summer of 1688, all four of John Goodwin's children had been seized by fits so severe that "it would have broke a heart of stone to have seen their agonies." Observing these "agonies" was a local minister named Cotton Mather, who agreed with the diagnosis offered by attending physician Thomas Oakes. The sudden onset, the inexplicable tantrums, the contagious hysteria—these signs could point only to witchcraft.

As with any "infectious disease," demonic possession was treated by tracing it to its source. In the case of the Goodwins, little sleuth work was required to reveal a probable suspect, for the children's trials had started soon after a hostile encounter with the mother of their washerwoman. The showdown began when thirteen-year-old Martha Goodwin interrogated the laundress about some linen that had gone missing. Infuriated by the implication that her daughter was a thief, Glover unleashed a hailstorm of "bad language" and verbal abuse upon the child, who promptly began to exhibit bizarre symptoms. The scourge soon spread to the three younger children, spurring Mather to offer his services as both avenger and exorcist.

Since a witch could only be convicted upon confession or the testimony of two witnesses, the minister's first step was establishing Glover's affinity for evil. After she proved unable to recite the Lord's Prayer intelligibly—a failure she attributed, in Gaelic, to her inability to understand English—Mather sealed her fate by securing a full confession through an interpreter. Further evidence was unearthed when the court searched her home, where several puppetlike dolls were deemed to be tools of the witches' trade. More damning still was the accused woman's delight when her possessions were brought to her in prison—delight that sparked a fresh wave of suffering for the Goodwin children when Glover was permitted to handle the dolls.

Satisfied that his suspicions were true, Mather visited Glover in her cell to find out more about the dark side and the demons that had recruited her. In one encounter, she reportedly referred to the devil as her prince and admitted to knowing four others who were in league with him. Despite these unwholesome associates, Glover agreed to pray with Mather in the days before her execution. And, in opposition to her supposed warnings to the Goodwins, her last recorded words were, "I die a Catholic"—a detail some have seen as proof that her only crime was allegiance to the "wrong" faith.

Whether aligned with the pope or the pagans, Glover was unlikely to find much sympathy with Mather and his followers. Having been persecuted for their dissent from the Anglican Church while in England, the Puritans were anxious to escape all vestiges of "popery" in the New World. This phobia of religious ritual was especially potent in Boston, where it took the form of an annual celebration known as Pope's Night. More of an organized riot than an actual observance, Pope's Night often culminated in the burning of effigies and attacks on local Catholics. As late as 1700, the General Court of Massachusetts passed a law commanding all Catholic priests to leave its borders within three months or face the death penalty. Obviously, the year 1688 was a bad time to be a Catholic in Boston, especially under the watchful gaze of ministers like Mather.

Since the only published account of the Goodwins' afflictions was authored by Mather himself, we have only his perspective on Glover's actions. If his version is to be believed, the children's symptoms were surreal enough to justify suspicions of satanic foul play. Barking like dogs, purring like cats, alternating between extremes of sweating and shivering, and even appearing to fly "with incredible swiftness through the air" were among the strange signs itemized in the minister's narrative. Not helping Glover's case was the fact that she had been accused of another instance of black magic six years earlier, when a woman confided on her deathbed that the crone had bewitched her. The sole witness to this startling revelation refused to testify when her own son was beset by a "black thing with a blue cap"—further evidence that Glover had demons at her disposal.

Despite these incriminating rumors an equally compelling case can be made that she was merely a Catholic in the wrong place at the wrong time. Her bungling of the Lord's Prayer is explained by her unfamiliarity with English, while her confession could easily have been fabricated by unscrupulous interpreters. The scandalous puppets may have been religious icons, and Mather himself admitted that she referred to the spirits that ruled her as "saints."

Had this rush to judgment been limited to one ornery old woman, Mather's actions might have been excused as the overreaction of a righteous soul. But when his name was linked to the witchcraft hysteria in Salem four years later, critics wondered if Glover's execution had been a sign of more terrible injustices to come. In Boston, however, the practice of witch hanging came to an end with Glover, who received a posthumous apology from the city in 1988, when the Boston City Council named the anniversary of her death (November 16) "Goody Glover Day."

COTTON MATHER AND THE
INOCULATION CONTROVERSY

~ 1721 ~

COTTON MATHER WOKE TO THE SOUND OF SHATTERING GLASS and rushed down the hall to his guest room, where a minister from Roxbury had been sleeping. He and the shaken minister looked from the jagged hole in the window to the grenade on the floor. The grenade had not detonated due to a collision with the casement, but a message attached to its fuse left no doubt about the intentions of the vandal who'd thrown it. Placed "so that it might outlive the breaking of the shell," the note read, "Cotton Mather, You Dog, Dam you: I'll Inoculate you with this, with a Pox to you."

Accustomed as we are to the miracles of modern health care, it's hard for us to grasp the extremity of an epidemic like the one that beset Boston in 1721, when Cotton Mather survived this assassination attempt. Known as the "speckled monster" because of the blemishes it left on its victims, smallpox was capable of "filling the churchyard with corpses, tormenting with constant fear all whom it had not yet stricken, leaving on those whose lives it spared the hideous traces of its power, turning the babe into a changeling at which the mother shuddered, and making the eyes and cheeks of the betrothed maiden objects of horror to the lover."

From blue-blooded Brahmins to recent immigrants from Ireland, no one was immune to this "grievous calamity," which was only exacerbated by the attentions of colonial doctors. Indeed, the symptoms of smallpox might have seemed tolerable when weighed against remedies like purging, bleeding, blistering, and the application of salves made of offal—all of which were in vogue when smallpox raged through the city that spring.

An unlikely opponent of these practices arose in the person of Mather, the Puritan minister who had spearheaded the Salem witch trials in 1682. Mather's progressive attitude toward medicine stood in marked contrast to his religious conservatism, which had driven him in his persecution of Quakers, Catholics, and other spiritual dissidents. Controversial as these crusades had been, his most unpopular campaign was his advocacy of inoculation, which turned many of his former supporters against him.

Mather's urgency in promoting the new science was underlined by the "terrors" of his two children, Sammy and Lizy, who begged him to intervene before the disease found its way into their home. Standing between the minister and his children's health was the incensed public, which subjected him to such "Outrages and Obloquies" that he felt he'd been "crucified with Christ."

In the end, Mather's obstinacy proved beneficial to the cause of inoculation, paving the way for future breakthroughs by Louis Pasteur and Edward Jenner. Such strides must have seemed unlikely in the throes of the 1721 plague, when many believed that disease was an instrument of God's judgment. Compounding this view was the understandable fear that inoculation, which involved "self-procuring the Small Pox," would backfire and fuel the fever's spread.

What motivated Mather, that staunch opponent of alternative religions, to stake his name on an experiment so radical? His exposure to inoculation came from two very different sources: the *Philosophical Transactions* of the Royal Society of London, the era's foremost scientific organization; and his slave Onesimus, a Coromantee from West Africa. From the journal, he learned of successful inoculations performed in Turkey, while Onesimus informed him of a similar practice among his people.

Boston's physicians, however, remained deaf to Mather's pleas, subscribing instead to the popular belief that inoculation would only spread the disease. Dr. Zabdiel Boylston was alone in his willingness to listen to Mather. On June 26, 1721, he deliberately infected three patients: an adult slave named Jack, a slave boy named Jackey, and Boylston's own six-year-old son, whose inclusion struck many as an act of reckless endangerment. After wounding the skin of each patient, Boylston applied a sample of active smallpox, causing each to receive a mild case of the dreaded disease. As risky as it must have seemed to laymen at the time, this procedure aimed to establish immunity by inflicting controlled infection.

From Boylston's decision to use his own son in the experiment, we may deduce that he harbored some optimism about its outcome. Equally confident was Mather, who opted to inoculate his own children soon afterward. Though the initial test subjects survived both the epidemic and the inoculation, Mather had a few dark nights of the soul when it seemed that Sammy "had . . . taken the Infection in the common Way" before the incision was administered. "If he should miscarry," the minister fretted in his diary, "besides the Loss of so hopeful a Son, I should also suffer a prodigious Clamour and Hatred from an infuriated Mob, whom the Devil has inspired . . . on this Occasion."

In the end, Mather's son survived and only 6 of the 247 people Boylston treated succumbed to the disease—an impressive statistic when weighed against the more than 840 lives eventually claimed by the epidemic in Boston. But opposition still remained violent, inspiring the diatribes of printer James Franklin (whose newspaper, the *Courant,* was founded as a forum for rants against inoculation) and leaving Boylston in fear for his life. Regardless of the successful results, many equated experimentation on the human body with playing God and consequently feared that to do so was to tempt God's wrath.

Mather's collaboration with Boylston is remarkable both for its consequences (the first successful immunization in the Western world) and for forging an alliance between religious faith and empirical science. Though their efforts were greeted with grenades and lynch mobs, the partners went on to earn international acclaim for their project. Mather's vindication came in 1723 when he was elected to the Royal Society, whose journal had inspired the experiment. The following year, Boylston traveled to England to address the Royal College of Physicians and Surgeons, where he was embraced as a pioneer in the fledgling specialty of immunization.

ELISHA BROWN BEATS
THE BRITISH ARMY

- 1768 -

Elisha Brown had not been granted many opportunities for leadership in his life. His humble lodgings—at the Manufactory House, a building founded as a factory for spinning and later adapted for use by private residents—reflected his disadvantaged circumstances, but such hardship didn't stop him from becoming a hero when the situation demanded one. For it was Elisha Brown who answered the door when the local sheriff showed up to take over the Manufactory House as an encampment for British soldiers. And it was Elisha Brown who slammed the door in the sheriff's face, triggering a standoff that would inflame the sympathies of Boston patriots while offering the British a preview of battles to come.

When Sheriff Stephen Greenleaf knocked on the door of the Manufactory House, the gesture was merely a formality. After all, the tenants were poor and powerless, and the property had been earmarked as a barracks for British troops. Though Greenleaf didn't expect a warm reception, he certainly expected the occupants to comply with the order. It was one thing for the town's leaders to deny access to public buildings and private homes, but certainly these lowly renters would have to cede their space to the British.

The occupants, led by Brown, were not amenable to this plan, however, and promptly barred the door against Greenleaf and the company of troops. Reacting quickly to this unforeseen obstacle, the soldiers surrounded the building in an attempt to starve the tenants out. The tables turned when the troops found themselves surrounded by townspeople, who tossed bread and other rations to the holdouts inside. Greenleaf's subsequent attempt to occupy the building backfired when he and his deputies broke into the basement, only to find themselves imprisoned there by Brown and his sympathizers.

Though the sheriff and his men were eventually rescued by a band of soldiers from Boston Common, the stalemate between Brown and the British army lasted for seventeen days. Eventually, the troops were pulled out by the governor who had sent them, marking the first figurative success of American colonists against armed British soldiers. Alone among these dissenters, Brown attained immortality for his refusal to forfeit the residence for use as British quarters—a stand for which he is remembered on his tombstone (in the Granary Burying Ground), which reads, "bravely and successfully opposed a whole British regt. in their violent attempt to force him from his legal Habitation."

The tenants' victory is all the more remarkable when one considers the context in which it was staged. The troops had been summoned to impose order in the wake of a recent riot, which Governor Francis Bernard viewed as an indication of more violent protests to come. It is an index of his anxiety that he eventually ordered four thousand soldiers—a staggering sum in light of the fact that Boston's entire population was about sixteen thousand.

What could have justified the decision to import a soldier for every four citizens? The initial catalyst was the English Parliament's passage of the Townshend Acts, which imposed duties on imported paper, glass, tea, lead, and paint. Preceded by the Sugar Act and the Stamp Act, this new slate of taxes was the Crown's latest effort to milk the colonies for monetary gain. Adding to the outrage was the fact that these acts had been passed without a meeting of the Massachusetts legislature, thereby subjecting the colonists to taxation without representation.

After a series of town meetings, the legislature reconvened under the leadership of Samuel Adams, who objected to the "infringements on . . . natural and constitutional rights" in a letter to the House of Representatives. The letter went the rounds of other colonial legislatures, motivating merchants in New York and Philadelphia to organize in opposition to imported goods.

Alarmed by the colonists' insubordination and their refusal to retract the so-called Circular Letter, Governor Bernard moved to dissolve the Massachusetts legislature. When deprived of this forum for political dissent, objectors expressed their anger in the streets. The situation eventually escalated into a full-scale riot, wherein the comptroller's house was stoned and a pleasure boat belonging to Joseph Harrison, the customs collector, was torched. Harrison's house was ransacked in the ensuing melee, which left him and his son battered and forced Governor Bernard to flee to his country estate in Roxbury.

However drastic the mob's actions, hindsight suggests that Bernard overstated them in his frantic request for troops. Bernard was a British climber who had contrived to improve his station through marriage (his wife was a cousin of the illustrious Lord Barrington) and colonial service—an ascent that could only be hindered by American resistance. In fact, his star had started to fall long before the passage of the Townshend Acts, leaving him stranded in a role he no longer had the authority to execute since he had lost all credibility in the state he was assigned to govern.

In light of his declining fortunes, the governor may well have exaggerated his accounts of the uprising, effectively bypassing moderate solutions in favor of military occupation. Whatever his motivation, the soldiers were summoned from New York and Ireland, with the first transports arriving on September 30, 1768. Winter was fast approaching by the time General Gage arrived on October 15, only to find that his troops had been rendered homeless.

Understandably alarmed by the sudden arrival of so many redcoats, Boston's leaders refused to offer lodging within town limits. The troops were permitted to set up camp on Castle Island, but Governor Bernard believed this outpost was too remote to ensure security. There was little hope of hospitality from townsfolk opposed to the recent rash of taxes, and to camp on Boston Common would be to risk hypothermia.

Faced with this predicament, the Manufactory House must have seemed like a miraculous solution. It had been established in 1754 as an early form of public housing, offering rooms to the working poor in exchange for the on-site manufacture of linen. These rooms were later leased to private tenants for a nominal fee, and one such tenant was Brown, whose modest income prohibited him from purchasing his own property. Among the building's few amenities were the industrial looms that remained in the basement—bulky contraptions that were of little use to the British soldiers during their brief imprisonment.

Lacking though they were in leverage and lofty connections, the residents of the Manufactory House had no dearth of supporters when under siege. The British troops were eventually forced to rent quarters at Faneuil Hall, and the episode spelled the end of Bernard's tenure as acting governor. The colonists' victory was achieved with few weapons and little bloodshed, establishing a precedent in which principles proved stronger than an army of thousands.

THE DEATH OF CHRISTOPHER SNIDER

- 1770 -

EBENEZER RICHARDSON SCARCELY AIMED when he fired his musket into the taunting crowd that had tracked him to his home in the North End. To his mind, he was firing in self-defense—though his attackers were armed with little more than rocks, snow, eggs, rotten produce, and anti-British insults. Had one of the rocks not shattered the window and grazed his wife, the Loyalist merchant might never have loaded the empty gun with bird shot. He might not have fired so recklessly, later shouting, "Damn their blood. I don't care what I've done." And when the smoke cleared and the mob parted, an eleven-year-old child might not have been bleeding on the street, felled by eleven pellets to the chest and abdomen.

That youthful victim was Christopher Snider (sometimes spelled Sneider or Seider), who perished from his "very dangerous wound" within hours of the shooting. His presence in the mob is explained by the fact that it was marketing day, when schools were closed and townsfolk gathered to do their shopping. On this particular day, marketing was complicated by the brewing controversy over importation, which had gripped Bostonians' passions since the passage of the hated Townshend Acts in 1767. Opposition to the taxes took shape in an organized boycott of British goods—a boycott the citizens were supporting when they stormed Richardson's home that February morning.

Richardson's actions had made him an obvious target for anti-importation anger. Unmoved by his fellow Americans' resistance to British taxes, he'd become an informer to local customs agents who reported infractions to the Crown. In addition to advising British officials which ships and shops were evading their duties, he made his sentiments public by coming to the aid of a Loyalist merchant, Theophilus Lillie. When a crowd gathered to protest Lillie's practices, Richardson incited them further by attempting to remove an effigy that hung over the door of Lillie's shop. The outraged protestors chased Richardson to his own house nearby, where he soon fired the shots that gave their movement its first martyr.

When Snider's injuries were discovered, the crowd stormed Richardson's door, undeterred by the fact that he was now swinging a sword. Once they had seized him, they seemed determined to "put a rope around his neck and execute him themselves," but on the advice of a Patriot leader (William Molineux), they settled for dragging him through the streets. Samuel Adams later had the boy's body removed to Faneuil Hall, and Richardson was arrested and charged with murder.

More than two thousand people attended Snider's funeral five days later; it was the largest funeral the colonies had ever seen. "Young as he was," wrote the *Boston Gazette,* "he died in his country's cause"—a cause that would gain further momentum with the Boston Massacre the following week.

Though the Massacre has come to symbolize the Revolution's early rumblings, Snider's death may have won more converts to the cause of patriotism. The boy's significance as a Revolutionary catalyst is illustrated by the fact that he shares a gravestone with Massacre victims Samuel Gray, Samuel Maverick, James Caldwell, Crispus Attucks, and Patrick Carr. On the stone, he is remembered as "the innocent, first victim of the struggles between the Colonists and the Crown, which resulted in Independence." Adding to his posthumous celebrity is an elegiac poem written by Phillis Wheatley, the first African American poet. Wheatley's lines echoed the sentiments inscribed on Snider's funeral pall, which read, "The serpent is lurking in the grass. The fatal dart is thrown. Innocence is nowhere safe." She likened the child to "Achilles in his mid career," cut down by a "Tory chief" who "waits the curses of the age to come."

But the course of justice was not as straight in real life as it was in Wheatley's verse, and Richardson spent only two years in jail before being pardoned by the Crown. He later surfaced in a respectable role at the Philadelphia customs service, though the *Boston Gazette* noted that Philadelphia proved "too hot" for this "Bird of Darkness" to fly under the radar for long. Having run from his foul reputation, he ultimately could not hide and was forced to flee in fear for his life when a public notice called on "all Lovers of Liberty" to produce him, "tarred and feathered, at the Coffee House, there to expiate his sins against his country by a public recantation."

In conjunction with the Massacre, the Richardson-Snider incident broadened the rift between Boston's Patriots and Loyalists. Few felt content to remain neutral now that a child had been killed. Parliament's hasty retraction of most of the Townshend Acts (the month after the Massacre) did little to quell the anger awakened by the bloodshed—especially when colonists learned that the duty on tea would remain in place.

More than three years passed before Bostonians rejected this leftover tax by dumping 342 chests of British tea into Boston Harbor.

But the table was set for the Boston Tea Party—and the historic upheaval that followed—when a young boy was caught in the crossfire of a much smaller conflict. Little is known about who Christopher Snider was in life, but in death he inspired allegiance from thousands, many of whom might otherwise have continued to tolerate the infringements of British rule.

A BOOKSELLER BLINDSIDES
THE BRITISH

- 1776 -

NO WHITE CHRISTMAS HAS EVER BEEN MORE WELCOME than the one that dawned on Fort George in 1775, reviving the flagging spirits of Colonel Henry Knox and his small band of supporters. Knox had been encamped at the southern end of Lake George for two weeks, accompanied by his brother William, 42 heavy sleds, 80 yoke of oxen, 120,000 pounds of artillery, and assorted soldiers and hired men.

This unorthodox sledding party had stalled in the early stages of a journey that would cover some three hundred miles, starting at the formerly British Fort Ticonderoga and ending on the outskirts of Boston. Its purpose, as pitched by Knox to an approving General Washington earlier that winter, was to supply the beleaguered Continental Army with the arsenal they needed to banish the British from Boston. But a journey of three hundred miles begins with a single step, and to move toward the prospect of a liberated Boston, Knox and his men needed enough snow to go sledding.

It was a mission many regarded as idealistic, formulated by a soldier with little experience. Only in a meritocracy like Washington's army could a twenty-five-year-old bookseller attain the rank of colonel, having trained himself for the role by reading exhaustively about military tactics. Knox's inexperience proved no impediment to his enthusiasm, however—an asset that made him more valuable to the rebels than the most seasoned veteran might have been.

His plan seemed simple on paper: Washington's depleted forces lacked the arms they needed to reclaim Boston from the redcoats. An embarrassment of arms was available at Fort Ticonderoga, which had been captured from the British by Ethan Allen and the Green Mountain Boys in May. Why not make an expedition to the abandoned fort and haul the artillery back to Boston? Once the weapons were installed on Dorchester Heights, with the British fleet in their sights, the enemy would have to retreat or risk being decimated by the Americans.

Washington signed off on the scheme at once, dispatching Knox and his nineteen-year-old brother on November 16, 1775. The brothers were given a budget of one thousand dollars with which to equip themselves. They began with a trip to the limestone fort on faraway Lake Champlain. Here they found enough weaponry to justify the miles they had traveled, including French mortars and a variety of heavy cannon. They wasted no time in starting the first phase of the return voyage, which required transporting the guns by boat before Lake George froze over.

Knox's entourage was beset by "the utmost difficulty" on the frigid lake, encountering relentless headwinds and making occasional stops to cut through the ice. When the eight-day crossing came to a close some forty miles south at Fort George, Knox wrote his wife that the worst of it was over. "We shall cut no small figure through the country with our cannon," he enthused, little knowing that his sledding party's momentum would soon be stopped by a sudden thaw.

Imagine his elation when snow began to fall on Christmas Day, smoothing the way for the overland journey to Albany. Stir crazy from the long layover on Lake George, Knox set forth on foot in a blizzard, nearly succumbing to hypothermia before opting to ride the rest of the way in a sleigh. The rest of the convoy remained at the fort until the snow let up and then caught up with the young colonel in Albany. After a second thaw on New Year's Day, the sleds began their foray across the frozen Hudson.

The expedition was set back yet again when one of the largest cannons broke through the ice, necessitating an all-day rescue effort aided by "the good people of . . . Albany." The next leg of the journey rivaled the Iditarod in difficulty, encompassing more than a hundred miles of mountain passes, untamed forest, and rough terrain. At one particularly dicey juncture in the Berkshires, some of the sled drivers refused to go forward, moving only after hours of impassioned persuasion from Knox.

The oxen were exchanged for horses in the trek's homestretch, which swung through the Massachusetts towns of Springfield, Brookfield, Spencer, Leicester, Worcester, Shrewsbury, Northborough, Marlborough, Southborough, Framingham, Wayland, Weston, Waltham, and Watertown. As news spread of the "noble train of artillery," spectators gathered to inspect the arsenal as it sped toward its destination. The guns were deposited twenty miles west of Boston while Knox hastened on to Cambridge, where he reported to Washington. Upon hearing that the visionary scheme had succeeded, the commander in chief put the bookseller in charge of the artillery, which would enable the Continental Army to attempt a strategy that "might put a final end to the war."

Six weeks later on March 5, 1776, the British awoke to find themselves in the sights of a fully stocked fortification on Dorchester Heights—one that had materialized overnight during a diversionary bombardment from Roxbury, Cobble Hill, and Lechmere Point. "My God," the British General William Howe reportedly said, "These fellows have done more work in one night than I could make my army do in three months."

And a long night it had been, in keeping with the rigors that had brought the guns from Ticonderoga to Dorchester. Hidden behind a hastily assembled barrier of hay bales, two thousand men had lugged supplies across the causeway and up the slopes to the summit of Dorchester Heights. After three or four trips with oxen-pulled carts and heavy wagons, they'd labored until dawn, constructing the fort from prefabricated timber frames and barrels of frozen earth. The resulting structure was equal parts execution and artifice; the barrels created an illusion of armor while the actual cannon were accompanied by logs painted to resemble additional artillery.

Comparing the Americans' masterstroke with the works of "the genie belonging to Aladdin's lamp," one prominent British officer wrote, "From these hills they command the whole town, so that we must drive them from their post, or desert the place." General Howe's initial plan to attack the fort was scuttled when a violent storm set in, bringing hail, sleet, snow, and hurricane-force winds. On March 18 the British began the evacuation of Boston, having been blindsided by a series of events stranger than the fiction stocked in Henry Knox's bookstore.

THE LAST STAND OF
CAPTAIN LAWRENCE

- 1813 -

BETWEEN THE SMOKE FROM THE LATEST BOMBARDMENT and the hordes of British soldiers boarding his ship, the crippled captain was barely visible to his crew when he issued his final order. Having sustained a shot to the leg and shrapnel wounds from a grenade blast, the American commander was finally felled by a bullet to the abdomen. But even as his men dragged him from the deck to nurse his fatal wound below, Captain Lawrence would not be silenced. "Tell the men to fire faster and not give up the ship," he exhorted his beleaguered sailors once more. "The colors shall wave while I live. Don't give up the ship!"

It was the outcome least expected by the audience of dinghies, sloops, pilot boats, fishing craft, and pleasure boats that had gathered off of Boston's Long Wharf at the battle's outset, waiting breathlessly as if for a championship prizefight: The American frigate *Chesapeake,* under the command of Master Commandant

Captain James Lawrence, had set forth for a skirmish with the *Shannon,* a British man-of-war helmed by Sir Philip Bowes Vere Broke. The spectators viewed the *Chesapeake* as a clear favorite, having been conditioned by eight months of American success against the British navy. Compounding the onlookers' confidence was the growing legend of Captain Lawrence, who had defeated the British brig *Peacock* in less than twelve minutes while commanding the American *Hornet.*

A similar rout was expected when the *Chesapeake* left shore to face the *Shannon.* The British ship had been circling Boston's harbor islands in plain view, spoiling for a fight with the American commander. Anxious to avenge the loss of the *Peacock,* Broke had issued a challenge to Lawrence, baiting him to fight "ship to ship, to try the fortunes of our respective flags." Though the combative letter was never received, Lawrence needed no such motivation to embark for Boston Light that day. As hundreds congregated on the headlands and cliffs of the mainland, a floating band of thrill seekers followed the *Chesapeake* to her engagement offshore.

It was evening by the time the two ships pulled abreast of each other. Several minutes elapsed between the sound of drums beating men to quarters and the first exchange of fire, which reduced the *Chesapeake*'s deck to a "cloud of splinters, hammocks, and other wreck." Though the subsequent battle was obscured by a scrim of yellow smoke, the onlookers may have heard Broke's order to "kill the men," which inspired a barrage from his sharpshooters. This volley wounded three American quartermasters and crippled Captain Lawrence, who continued to direct the battle with a musket ball in one leg.

After a hand grenade demolished one of the *Chesapeake*'s quarterdeck arms chests, the captain remained on deck, exhorting his men to board the British ship even as his own was engulfed in flames. When the smoke cleared from the grenade blast, a British lieutenant spotted Lawrence leaning on the companionway and fired at him. This shot would prove fatal both for Lawrence and the ship he'd so valiantly commanded, necessitating his removal to a cabin below—and his stirring last order—just as the British began streaming over the sides of the *Chesapeake.*

In the final throes of the battle, a dying American sailor swiped desperately at Captain Broke, who was armed solely with a sword. The cutlass blow landed on the commander's head, severing part of his skull and rendering him delirious for the triumphant trip to Halifax, Nova Scotia (headquarters of England's naval fleet), where both the *Shannon* and the captured *Chesapeake* were steered with the British flag at their mastheads.

Miraculously, Broke survived his critical head wound, but Captain Lawrence succumbed to his injuries en route, and his first lieutenant, Augustus C. Ludlow, died soon after arrival. The Americans were honored with a full naval funeral in Halifax, and their remains were later interred in the cemetery at New York's Trinity Church. Lawrence's headstone repeats the utterance that later became the motto of the United States Navy, reading, "Neither the fury of battle, the anguish of a mortal wound, nor the horrors of approaching death could subdue his gallant spirit. His dying words were, 'Don't give up the Ship.'"

THE UNTIMELY DEMISE
OF DAVID WALKER

- 1829 -

YOU DON'T HAVE TO BE A CONSPIRACY THEORIST TO SUSPECT foul play in the untimely death of David Walker. Less than a year had elapsed between the publication of *An Appeal to the Coloured Citizens of the World* and the discovery of its author's body in his Beacon Hill home—a period in which Walker had fielded a decade's worth of death threats.

An imposing figure in life with his "slender and well proportioned physique," he was in his mid-forties when he died, clad as always in the modest style in which he specialized as a clothier. Lacking DNA evidence to unravel the mystery, it may never be known whether the African-American abolitionist was poisoned or succumbed to natural causes.

Had murder been proven, the potential suspects would have been legion. Southern plantation owners reacted to the *Appeal* by offering a three thousand dollars bounty for Walker's death. The bloodlust behind this prize was in no way tempered by the simultaneous offer of ten thousand dollars should he be brought to the South alive. Though the outraged slaveholders surely wanted the author dead, they would have been most satisfied if they could make an example of him before killing him and themselves.

Whether his death was caused by a seizure, tuberculosis, or enemy intervention, a close reading of Walker's writing indicates that he was no stranger to the concept of a martyr's end. His preference for the grave over a life in chains provides some of the *Appeal's* most powerful passages, indicating the extremes to which he would go in defense of black freedom. "Had I not rather die, or be put to death," he wrote, "than to be a slave to any tyrant, who takes not only my own, but my wife and children's lives by the inches? Yea, would I meet death with avidity far! far!! in preference to such servile submission to the murderous hands of tyrants."

Though Walker himself was born free, to a free mother and a slave father, he had occasion to witness the evils of slavery before leaving the "bloody land" in which he was raised. Among the unutterable cruelties he'd seen in the South was an incident in which an enslaved son was forced to whip his own mother to death. With images like this engraved on his consciousness, it's no surprise that, when Walker turned to protest, his attitude was all or nothing.

It was the radicalism of the *Appeal* that alarmed slaveholders and others sympathetic to their cause, goading Southern officials to stop at nothing in suppressing it. The seventy-six-page pamphlet caused a commotion among citizens on both sides of the controversy; it radicalized abolitionists who had previously preferred moderation and it provoked slavery's profiteers to harden their defenses. Walker's thesis, much simplified, was that African Americans had been brought to "wretchedness" by the institution of slavery and its poisonous fruits—and immediate, unconditional, and universal emancipation offered the only solution.

More inflammatory still was his implication that violent means were justified in the pursuit of so just a cause. Invoking the principle of an eye for an eye, Walker exhorted his black readers to "kill or be killed . . . and believe this, that it is no more harm for you to kill a man who is trying to kill you, than it is for you to take a drink of water when thirsty." Read in its entirety, the *Appeal* can be seen as a call for black rebellion, and a warning to whites that "there is an unconquerable disposition in the breasts of the blacks, which, when it is fully awakened and put in motion, will be subdued only with the destruction of the animal existence."

It's a tribute to the potency of Walker's prose that Southerners treated his book as a ticking time bomb, scrambling to banish it at any cost. When sixty copies were confiscated in Savannah, Georgia— having been sewn into the linings of coats sold by Walker and smuggled into the South by Boston sailors—local officials barred black seamen from coming ashore at their port. In New Orleans, four black men were arrested for possession of the book, while whites in Walker's hometown of Wilmington, North Carolina, reacted by randomly persecuting free blacks. Not content to eradicate existing copies of the *Appeal,* legislatures in Georgia, Louisiana, and North Carolina sought to strangle black activism at its source, making it a crime to teach blacks how to read and write.

Though the book's fallout in the South was mainly negative, Walker's argument galvanized the passive abolitionist movement in the North. Though he found few converts—at least among whites— willing to embrace his vision of a violent uprising, his "impassioned and determined effort" found favor with prominent figures including William Lloyd Garrison, editor of the influential abolitionist newspaper the *Liberator.* Garrison became markedly less compromising after the publication of the *Appeal,* retracting his support for colonization (a movement advocating the resettlement of blacks in

Africa) and pushing instead for immediate emancipation. Walker's ideological heirs include Henry H. Garnet, Malcolm X, and Martin Luther King Jr., but his immediate impact was to incite contemporaries against the "insupportable insult" of slavery.

Boston was by no means exemplary where race relations were concerned, but it was a far preferable home for Walker than North Carolina in the early nineteenth century. Amid the controversy ensuing from the *Appeal's* debut, Mayor Josiah Quincy rejected repeated demands from Georgia and South Carolina, whose leaders petitioned him to arrest Walker and appropriate all published copies of the book. Walker didn't live to see the day when the South Carolina militia attacked Fort Sumter in Charleston, igniting the war that eventually banished slavery from American soil. But in the intervening decades between his death and the defeat of the Confederacy, his words would resonate from New England drawing rooms to Georgian slave quarters, removing apathy as an option for all who read them.

LAURA BRIDGMAN SPEAKS

- 1837 -

HER FIRST WORDS WERE FOR SIMPLE HOUSEHOLD OBJECTS she was able to identify through labels and eventually name in the newly learned language of finger spelling. But even in her fledgling grasp of books, spoons, boots, tables, and flowers, Laura Bridgman had eclipsed the efforts of every deaf-blind student Samuel Gridley Howe had ever taught. Her understanding went beyond rote repetition as "the truth began to flash upon her, [and] her intellect began to work." When the child "perceived that here was a way by which she could herself make a sign of anything that was in her own mind . . . her countenance lighted up." It was a moment of triumph and vindication for the man who had tutored her, the ineffable "moment when this truth dawned upon her mind, and spread its light to her countenance."

Laura Bridgman was merely seven years old when she experienced this breakthrough with Howe, and within months she'd become a fluent finger speller with a seemingly bottomless thirst for knowledge. Perhaps language came easily because Laura had spoken before. Before she contracted the disease that robbed her of her sight and hearing, she'd been a precocious talker, capable of expressing herself in sentences even at twenty months.

At two years old, she was stricken with the scarlet fever that disabled her, leaving only her sense of touch intact. Though lucky to have survived a disease that killed her two older sisters, she was effectively stranded during the years between the onset of the fever and her "discovery" by Samuel Gridley Howe, the charismatic director of the Perkins Institution for the Blind. As the oldest child of a New Hampshire farming family, she was often left to her own devices, addressed only through the occasional pat on the back or face. Her overburdened mother, though affectionate, "could not dream of how to encourage or comfort [her] much" and was somewhat relieved to entrust her to Howe's care.

As for Howe, he had long searched for a suitable student on whom to test his theory that the deaf-blind could be educated, and Laura impressed him as a raw canvas with the potential to become a masterpiece. Thus began a relationship that would attract international fame for Laura and elevate Howe to the status of "rationalist redeemer." Using raised alphabets, finger spelling, embossed labels, and other innovative techniques, he shepherded his protégée toward a breakthrough that uncaged her "immortal spirit, eagerly seizing upon a new link of union with other spirits!"

Such was the sway of Laura's story that she became an international celebrity, with spectators converging on the Perkins Institution by the thousands to witness the spectacle of her education. In 1842, her fame was sealed by a visit from an even bigger star: the novelist Charles Dickens, who swung through Boston on a two-week tour of American charitable institutions and literary salons. Though his whirlwind schedule included stops at the House of Reformation for Juvenile Offenders, the Massachusetts House of Correction, the

Boylston School for Neglected and Indigent Boys, and the State Hospital for the Insane, only one local institution was immortalized in *American Notes,* his popular record of the journey. This paragon of progress was the Perkins Institution, where he encountered a "fair young creature" who left him "more truly and deeply affected" than he had ever been in his life.

By the time Dickens visited her, Laura Bridgman had lived at Perkins for more than four years. During that period, she'd become the first deaf-blind person to learn language and master the ability to communicate with others—an achievement that cemented Boston's reputation as the Athens of America, along with Howe's growing status as a savior to the disabled.

Dickens himself could have scarcely dreamed up two characters more distinctive than the director and his star pupil. When the Boston-born Howe assumed the directorship of the Perkins Institution, he was already a veteran of the Greek revolution of the 1820s. Though he would retain his position until the end of his life, he had an insatiable appetite for causes—among them Polish independence, prison reform, nonsectarian education, and abolitionism.

These involvements notwithstanding, Howe's success with Laura remained his defining accomplishment, and one that earned him the admiration of contemporaries ranging from Thomas Carlyle to Florence Nightingale. His zeal for reformist causes was complicated by his restless ambition, which made him easily bored with his day job and the deskbound tasks that went with it. As moonlighting and overseas travel consumed more and more of his energy, Howe grew progressively more distant from the pupil he'd once regarded as his own daughter.

For Laura, her "salvation" at the hands of Howe was a mixed blessing. Though she agreed with his assessment that the gift of language had been a "joyous privilege," he also introduced her to a paradise she would later lose when he lost interest in her. Described as a sprightly, winsome toddler before the fever, the Laura that arrived at Perkins was a lonely, emotionally perceptive little girl. Once she regained her ability to converse through finger spelling, her quest for knowledge was matched only by her craving for affectionate companionship.

At the peak of her fame, Laura was Boston's biggest tourist attraction. Her emergence from the "darkness and silence of the tomb" was seen as proof of education's transformative power, while her upbeat demeanor in the face of affliction made her an icon of moral uplift. In Howe's published annual reports for Perkins, she was no less than a "lamp set upon a hill, whose light cannot be hid." And Dickens, not to be outdone, suggested that the child possessed virtues that could humble the "self-elected saints with gloomy brows."

The mission of the Perkins Institution reflects the rise of reform in nineteenth-century Boston, as Brahmin "haves" turned their attention to the aid and empowerment of "have-nots." Among those targeted by this philanthropic trend were orphans, prisoners, the elderly, the ill, the disabled, the indigent, the insane, and others previously left behind by society. The rise of humanitarianism would find its ultimate expression in the abolitionist movement, which would attract many of the same names (among them Howe and his wife, Julia Ward Howe) that haunted Perkins during Laura's tenure there.

If Laura resented her status as a mascot for the ideals of her era, she kept her feelings to herself. Her fame, like that of so many child celebrities, ran its course by the time she reached adolescence, and she was eventually all but forgotten in favor of a second, more compelling Perkins student: Helen Keller. In her heyday, Laura was exalted by Carlyle as an "angel-soul" and imbued by Dickens with a "healing touch akin to that of the Great Master," but these words of praise were no substitute for the sustaining relationships that seemed to elude her all her life.

ARSON AT THE URSULINE CONVENT

- 1834 -

THE SISTERS AND STUDENTS MADE A PITIFUL SIGHT as they collapsed in the rooms of their temporary protector, Joseph Adams of Winter Hill. The older nuns struggled to stay calm for the children, who had been rousted from their beds with the news that the Ursuline Convent was on fire. The students had scarcely had time to dress before being shepherded to the garden, throwing on petticoats over their nightgowns and bonnets over their nightcaps. With bare legs and soiled slippers, the shivering refugees followed the nuns and Joseph Adams to his top floor to watch the convent burn.

From their vantage point a half mile away, they saw the windows of rooms they had recently vacated fill with flames. Overcome by the red sky over Charlestown and the rioters raging beneath it, they retreated to the parlor to pray, asking God to "forgive our sins as we forgive these unfortunate fanatics." Forgiveness, however, was the last thing on the vandals' minds as they swept over the nunnery's spacious grounds, laying waste to every last building and later returning to raze the orchards and fields.

The conflagration was observed by several fire companies from Boston and Charlestown, whose engines stood idle as the mob swarmed over Mount Benedict, where the convent was located. Had the residents remained cowering in the shadows of the mausoleum where they'd initially hidden, they would have witnessed looters invading the mortuary chapel. Lacking living objects for their anger, the men upended the coffins and urns of the sisters interred there, scattering ashes, emptying bodies onto the ground, and even pocketing teeth they had wrested from the corpses.

The desecration of the dead was the crowning atrocity of an evening that had started with "a dense black mass" of men converging on the convent. Led by a barrel-chested bricklayer named John R. Buzzell, the men began to light bonfires outside the gate. Their ostensible reason for gathering was suspicion over a recent rumor regarding Sister Mary John (nee Elizabeth Harrison), a nun who had fled the convent for the home of a neighboring Protestant. In a state of derangement possibly brought on by exhaustion, she refused repeated pleas to return to the Ursulines—a stance she later retracted when she'd come to her senses.

Though Harrison eventually returned to the convent on her own volition, the story of her "escape" had been sensationalized in a *Boston Mercantile Journal* article that implied she remained at the convent as a captive. Soon after the article's publication, anti-Catholic placards began to appear around Charlestown, and many residents began demanding a full investigation of this "mysterious affair," threatening the demolition of the nunnery at the hands of "the truckmen of Boston."

For those inclined to believe it, the Harrison rumor only confirmed the gothic legends that had been circulating about the Ursulines— among them legends of brutal penance, systematic deprivation, kidnapping schemes, and strange rituals, itemized in a tell-all memoir titled *Six Months in a Convent.* The memoir was written by Rebecca Reed, a former student of the convent, whose romantic fascination with a nun's life had soured upon exposure to its rigors. As the mother superior, Sister Mary Edmond St. George (nee Mary Anne Moffatt), observed in a rebuttal to the memoir, "The novelty of the scene wore away, and the hours she imagined she would spend with so much delight . . . she found, to her sorrow, appropriated by the duties of every day life."

Whatever the motive for Reed's allegations, her book exacerbated anti-Catholic prejudice in Boston, where Brahmins and working-class laborers alike were alarmed by an influx of Irish Catholic immigrants. The Massachusetts Bay Colony had been founded on a phobia of "popery," and Boston remained an inhospitable place to be Catholic in 1834. Despite this lingering bias, an Ursuline education was all the rage among Boston's Protestant elite, many of whose daughters enjoyed the benefits of cloistered schooling without the Catholicism that generally went with it.

By enrolling the city's aristocracy (who approved of the convent's methods, if not its overall mission), the Ursulines had hit on an ingenious method for funding the Catholic agenda in Boston with Protestant tuition. This "Catholic conspiracy" was the subject of several shrill lectures by Reverend Lyman Beecher, who'd visited Boston the day before the riot to raise funds for his own Protestant seminary. Dismissing the education of Protestants by Catholics as "gratuitous," he warned of "Romish" schools preying on Protestant offspring "while the subjects of the Pope were left to roam in ignorance, many of them incapable of either reading or writing."

Beecher was preaching to the converted where the "truckmen of Boston" were concerned, providing moral justification for resentment that was equal parts religious, racial, and financial. To the bricklayers, sailors, firefighters, and other laborers that took part in the arson, the convent was a symbol of education their own children could never afford, rituals their forefathers had struggled to escape, and immigrants (the Irish) whose inflow made a poor economy worse.

Ethnic and economic incentives remained unspoken when the posse marched up the hill to mass outside the convent's door, summoning the mother superior and ordering her to produce "the nun that ran away." Considering the situation's volatility, St. George certainly didn't do herself any favors when she refused, scolding them for disturbing the sleeping daughters of the city's most prominent citizens. Adding fuel to the flames, she warned them to "disperse immediately, for if you don't, the Bishop has twenty thousand Irishmen at his command in Boston, and they will whip you all into the sea!"

After adjourning to the bottom of the hill to paint their faces and distribute torches, the mob returned to the door with cries of "Down with the Pope! Down with the Bishops! Down with the Convent!" As the sisters woke the students and herded them into the garden, the men broke down the front door and began a rampage that seemed to escalate with every assault. Their fury sustained itself until sunrise, leaving furniture splintered, china shattered, books burned, and musical instruments gutted.

At the riot's apex, Buzzell donned the bishop's robes and presided over a bonfire fueled by bibles, crosses, religious vestments, altar ornaments, and other sacramental items. He was abetted by a sixteen-year-old boy named Marvin Marcy, who assumed the pose of an auctioneer while feeding the flames with religious texts. "Going once," the youth would shout to the crowd before pronouncing a book "sold" and consigning it to the pyre.

Between fifty and two hundred men participated in the ransacking and arson that night, attended by a crowd of more than a thousand onlookers. Only thirteen men were eventually arrested and tried, and of those, only the youngest, Marvin Marcy, was convicted and sentenced to life imprisonment. John Buzzell later boasted that he'd known he would never pay for his crimes, despite the fact that "the testimony against me was point blank and sufficient to have convicted twenty men."

Despite this astonishing miscarriage of justice, St. George intervened on behalf of Marcy, signing a successful petition to have his sentence commuted. Though the Catholic archdiocese sued the state for an estimated fifty thousand dollars in damages, no redress was ever made, and the Ursuline school was not reestablished in Charlestown. The ruins of the convent remained on Mount Benedict for the following four decades, left there by the Catholic Church as a reproach to those whose intolerance had destroyed it. By the time it was sold in 1875, successive waves of immigration had changed the complexion of the city forever, leaving nearly half of its population Irish and ushering in the decline of Protestant dominance.

INAUGURATING THE ETHER DOME

- 1846 -

THE OPERATING THEATER WAS NEARLY EMPTY as Dr. John Collins Warren prepared for surgery. As in most major hospitals, Massachusetts General staged its surgeries under a spacious dome on the top floor. This was not because of the natural light or the architectural appeal, but rather because a dome was more likely to absorb the sound of patients screaming.

Warren's patient that day was a twenty-something housepainter named Gilbert Abbott. He had been admitted with a large tumor on the side of his neck, which the surgeon prepared to remove in the usual way—he would expose the "torturous, indurated veins" by dissection, cutting "sufficiently to enable . . . a ligature to be passed around them." When Abbott was instructed to remain sitting for the procedure, he assumed this was for the usual reason: What need was there to lie down, after all, if he would be conscious while the scalpel did its work?

But there would be no screaming in the room that morning, nor would Abbott feel any pain from the operation he was about to endure. Moments after 10:00 A.M., when the procedure was scheduled to begin, Warren addressed the few observers in the gallery. "Since many of you have not been informed for what purpose you're assembled here, I shall now explain it to you," he said, with uncharacteristic enthusiasm. "There is a gentleman who claims the inhalation of a certain agent will produce insensibility to pain during surgical operations, with safety to the patient. I have always considered this an important desideratum in operative surgery, and after due consideration I have decided to permit him to try the experiment."

Warren couldn't have created more of a sensation if he'd said he was going to raise the dead. In the mid-eighteenth century, surgery was synonymous with pain—so much so that it was not unusual for patients to die of shock on the operating table. The available options for pain relief were problematic, ranging from opium to hypnotism. Many preferred to drink heavily and hope for the best. If Warren's experiment was a success, it would be celebrated both as a medical milestone and a humanitarian triumph.

But to succeed, the operation had to take place, and the young dentist whose "agent" Warren had prepared to administer was nowhere to be found. As the clock moved toward 10:25, Warren faced the gallery and said curtly, "It appears that he is otherwise engaged." He then turned to the linen-draped table where his instruments were arrayed. The audience's mood was muted as Abbott braced himself for the first cut. Seeing a patient tortured in the name of healing was all in a day's work for these doctors and medical students, but Warren had led them to believe they'd witness history in the making.

No one was as disappointed as the doctor himself, who had long wished for "some means of lessening the sufferings he was obliged to inflict." To find it, he'd been willing to risk his reputation on a maverick named William T. G. Morton, whose modest credentials he'd have scoffed at under any other circumstances. Now it seemed that Morton had abandoned him at the eleventh hour, leaving him in the laughable position of promoting a hypothesis that couldn't be proved.

Yet when Morton strode into the room, muttering excuses about last-minute modifications to his equipment, Mass General's chief of surgery stepped aside and said, "Well, sir, your patient is ready." The sixty-eight-year-old Warren hadn't risen to the pinnacle of his profession by subjecting his patients to unproven methods, but Morton's claims were just too tantalizing to resist.

The observers returned to the edge of their seats as Morton filled a glass globe with his mysterious compound and advised Abbott to inhale its contents. It took only a few minutes for Abbott to become unconscious, and minutes more for Warren to make the necessary incisions. He completed the dissection, he later wrote in his journal, "without any expression of pain on the part of the patient." The operation's silence was broken only by Abbott's regular breathing and the occasional utterances of the surgeons. It was a silence that would soon be heard around the world, as doctors seized on the once impossible dream of substituting sleep for unspeakable pain.

Morton's secret substance was none other than sulfuric ether, which he'd mixed with orange oil to mask the scent of the ether. The inspiration for the experiment had come from a fellow dentist named Horace Wells, who'd discovered that nitrous oxide could ease the pain of extractions and other dental procedures. Wells, too, had been granted an audition with Warren the previous year, but he'd been denounced as a purveyor of "humbug" when the gas failed to fully subdue the patient.

Convinced that Wells was onto something, Morton set about finding a more potent gas. Though it's debatable whether his decision to try ether was his own or a theft from another doctor, he was advised on its usage by Dr. Charles Jackson, a Massachusetts Brahmin who also claimed to have conceived the telegraph (an invention attributed to Samuel Morse). Jackson would later contend that the discovery of ether's pain-relieving properties was entirely his own, while Wells's backers touted him as the founder of inhalation anesthetics.

The controversy grew when it came to light that the opportunistic Morton had taken out a patent on his so-called compound, putting a premium on its usage just as word began to spread about its effectiveness. Dubbing the mixture "Letheon," he planned to exact a fee from every medical and dental facility that used it to alleviate suffering. Though the patent would eventually prove useless when the "compound" was revealed to be ether (along with the superfluous scent of orange), Morton had set a precedent for a practice that would eventually become prevalent: the exploitation of medical discovery for monetary gain.

In Boston's Public Garden, a statue by John Q. A. Ward immortalizes October 16, 1847, as the date of the "death of pain." Due to the unresolved conflict between Morton, Wells, and Jackson, no name is credited for the discovery. Whoever was ultimately responsible for it, etherization opened the door for modern anesthesia, subtracting the dread from surgical procedures and allowing medicine to advance beyond the obstacles posed by extreme pain.

BOSTONIANS STRIKE A BLOW
AGAINST THE FUGITIVE SLAVE ACT

- 1850 -

When Dr. Samuel Gridley Howe appeared at his door that night, Reverend Theodore Parker knew it was not a social call. Parker set aside the sermon he was writing and steeled himself for bad news. There'd been no shortage of things to panic about since the passage of the Fugitive Slave Act in September, and Howe's grave expression promised more of the same.

Once settled in the study, Howe relayed the information he'd gathered from a sympathetic spy in the United States Marshals office. A Georgian slave catcher named Willis Hughes had breached Boston's borders, accompanied by a cabinetmaker named John Knight. The pair had come to retrieve two runaway slaves named Ellen and William Craft, and they were equipped with warrants for the Crafts' arrest and immediate return to bondage.

Even two months before, Howe and Parker might have yawned at the idea of slave catchers in their midst. Boston's abolitionist leaders prided themselves on having protected countless fugitives from capture—so much so that the Crafts had heard "no slave hunter has ever been able to get a slave out of Boston."

But those odds were bound to change in the aftermath of the Fugitive Slave Act, which made harboring slaves a crime punishable by six months in jail and a one-thousand-dollar fine. If the abetted slave escaped, anyone who helped was required to compensate the owner with a second one thousand dollar check. Furthermore, should an escaped slave ever make it to the courtroom, he was barred from testifying on his own behalf.

Howe and Parker had no intention of letting Ellen and William be dragged into court, where the law decreed that a judge be paid ten dollars to decide a defendant was a slave, and only five dollars should he deem the accused to be free. In a biased system such as this, a trial would be little more than a formality between the Crafts' capture and their consignment to a marshal, who would return them to Macon, Georgia, and the masters they had escaped.

"We must hide William and Ellen until we get rid of the slave catchers," Parker said, enlisting Howe's help in finding a suitable hiding place and sending Hughes home empty-handed. They had a network of supporters to rely on, thanks to Parker's status as chairman of Boston's Vigilance Committee. The committee had been founded soon after President Millard Fillmore's passage of the Fugitive Slave Act and had since raised the funds to assist more than one hundred runaway slaves. The Crafts were among the first to need the committee's aid in escaping would-be captors, and their plight sparked a flurry of activity among local abolitionists.

William and Ellen had already gotten wind of the plot to capture them by the time the Vigilance Committee mobilized on their behalf. William had received a suspicious visitor at the cabinetry shop where he worked—an unwelcome face from his past named John

Knight. Knight was a white carpenter who had worked with William in Macon, where William was required to build furniture while his master claimed his wages. Because of his ability to identify the Crafts, Knight had been enlisted as a traveling companion for Hughes, who had never met most of the people he set out to capture.

Thankfully, William was far too perceptive to believe Knight's claim that he just happened to be in Boston. Deflecting the visitor's requests to show him the town, William left the shop and bought a revolver for protection. He was not a violent man, but he and Ellen had come too far to be sent back to a situation in which they could never marry or have children, knowing they could be sold away from each other just as their families had been sold away from them.

To escape the bleak future that lay ahead of them in Macon, the Crafts had hatched a daring and ingenious plan in the winter of 1848. Capitalizing on the fact that Ellen, who was the product of an exploitative relationship between a slave master and his slave, was fair enough to pass for white, they decided she should don the disguise of a white gentleman and book passage to Philadelphia. The reason for this temporary sex change was that a white woman would never travel alone with a male slave, but a man would attract no notice when attended by a slave like William.

And so it was that Ellen, in a top hat and trousers, boarded the first-class compartment of a train bound for Savannah, while William stowed her luggage and retreated to the slave car. As a final precaution, she obscured her face with a bandage and contrived a makeshift sling for her arm. These touches offered added assurance that her gender wouldn't be betrayed by the smoothness of her skin, and that she'd have an excuse to fall back on if someone asked her to sign her name. Neither Ellen nor William was able to read or write at the time, like so many others who'd been affected by Southern laws against educating slaves.

After a perilous journey, William and Ellen arrived in Boston, having been sent by a Philadelphian abolitionist who told them of Parker and his powerful friends. Over the ensuing months, the couple had ample exposure to these and other champions of emancipation, developing close ties to Parker, whose parishioners they became. Now the promises that had lured them to "the cradle of liberty" would be put to the test: Would the abolitionists stand strong even in the face of fines and imprisonment?

The succession of helpers that rallied to the Crafts' defense had to do so despite resistance, as the couple was opposed to risking the reputations and security of others. Three separate families harbored the fugitives until it was decided they'd be safer if they separated, with William going to the home of Lewis Hayden while Ellen resided under Parker's roof.

Meanwhile, members of Boston's Vigilance Committee treated Hughes and Knight to the town's peculiar brand of hospitality, labeling them "Slave Hunters" in printed posters and pursuing them through the streets chanting, "Go back to Georgia!" The committee's lawyers even issued a warrant for Hughes's arrest, charging him with slander and conspiracy to kidnap. In the end, it was the slave catcher who was forced to appear in court, earning his freedom only after a local merchant paid the staggering sum of ten thousand dollars for his bail.

If not for Parker, Hughes may never have escaped Boston with his life, much less his liberty. Though the pacifist minister had grown accustomed to guarding Ellen with a gun at his side, he intervened when an angry black man brandished a revolver after Hughes's trial. "I will not let you have his murder on your conscience!" he told the potential assassin, promising that the slave catcher would be leaving Boston the following morning. And leave he and Knight did, but not without a prodding visit from Parker, who told them he could not vouch for their safety if they stayed another night.

When the empty-handed slave catchers made their exit on an afternoon train, the Crafts knew that the battle had been won but the war was just beginning. As long as the Fugitive Slave Act was in place, they would never be safe on American soil—not even in Boston, where their friends would undoubtedly be penalized for protecting them.

The following April in Boston, a fugitive slave named Thomas Sims was returned to Georgia despite abolitionists' best efforts to free him. Others would follow, but by that time the Crafts had resettled in England, where they had fled with assistance from Parker. Before leaving, they asked the minister to perform one final favor by pronouncing them man and wife. The wedding was a symbol of a hope they had never dared harbor in Georgia: the hope that their union would flourish in a place where freedom was the birthright of every human, and not just those who happened to be born white.

THE MASSACHUSETTS
FIFTY-FOURTH GOES TO WAR

- 1863 -

SINCE THE START OF THE CIVIL WAR IN 1860, Bostonians had grown accustomed to seeing off soldiers on their way to the front. Countless regiments of cavalry, infantry, and artillery had marched through the cobblestone streets to the waterfront, brandishing their polished rifles as onlookers applauded from the sidelines. But the turnout was unusually high for the procession scheduled on May 28, and the atmosphere was especially electric. All of abolitionist Boston was out in force for this particular parade, because the company they had come to honor was the first African-American regiment to take up arms for the Union.

Under the canopy of a clear blue sky, the thousand soldiers of the Massachusetts Fifty-fourth strode into view, accompanied by an advance guard of police. Mounted riders, two bands, and a drum corps led the procession, ushering in the men who would serve as a symbol of the war's new direction. In January of that year, President

Abraham Lincoln had signed the Emancipation Proclamation, enforcing his decree that all slaves in seceded states would be "then, thenceforward, and forever free."

The Fifty-fourth was the realization of the Proclamation's fine print, which authorized former slaves to be accepted into the armed forces. The regiment was also a reflection of Massachusetts's reputation as an abolitionist stronghold, having been marshaled into existence by the state's Republican, Free-Soiler governor, John Andrew. Perceiving the powerful impact black soldiers would have on a nation fatigued by war and beset by doubts, Andrew had ordered the enlistment of troops to serve as "a model for all future colored regiments."

He assigned the command of this exemplary corps to a member of one of Boston's elite families, a soldier "of the highest tone and honor" from the "circles of educated, antislavery society." This paragon was Robert Gould Shaw, the twenty-six-year-old son of impassioned progressives Francis George Shaw and Sarah Blake Sturgis Shaw.

Despite the ardent abolitionism of his parents, Shaw was less committed to the cause than many of the other white officers in his regiment. Even so, he realized the gravity of the role in which he'd been cast and understood Andrew's admonition that the Fifty-fourth's performance would, in large part, determine "the estimation in which the character of . . . colored Americans [would] be held throughout the world."

If the soldiers themselves were unaware of the weight of history on their shoulders, it was not for lack of reminders. From recruitment to receipt of their regimental colors, they had been repeatedly impressed with their status as the standard-bearers of their race. The ultimate expression of this message came on May 18, when they assembled for a presentation of four flags symbolizing their mission. In the presence of abolitionist leaders including Frederick Douglass,

Lewis Hayden, and William Lloyd Garrison, Andrew exhorted them to "strike a blow" for black freedom, saying, "I know not . . . when, in all human history, to any given thousand men in arms there has been committed a work at once so proud, so precious, so full of hope and glory as the work committed to you."

The free blacks and emancipated slaves of the Fifty-fourth would prove equal to the expectations invested in them, performing so valiantly in their first skirmish that a member of the Tenth Connecticut Infantry wrote, "But for the bravery of . . . the Massachusetts Fifty-fourth (colored), our whole regiment would have been captured. They fought like heroes." By all accounts, the regiment had not only reversed the popular prejudice that accused black men of laziness and lack of discipline, but it had also established itself as a superior unit by any standards—one whose courage and commitment set an example for every soldier.

Despite this excellence, the black soldiers were being paid laborers' wages rather than the equal compensation they'd been promised by recruiters. While white soldiers collected a flat fee of thirteen dollars a month, members of the Fifty-fourth were paid ten dollars, from which three dollars was subtracted for clothing and other expenses. Rather than accept this inequity and the disrespect it implied, the men refused the reduced paychecks as a form of protest. By the time the government would amend its decision the following year, many of the soldiers who had fought without pay would be dead.

Those watching Colonel Shaw and his soldiers on May 28 had no inkling of what their fate would be as they marched from Boston Common to Battery Wharf. To some, the regiment had served its purpose merely by existing, and thereby validating the moral imperative set forth in the Emancipation Proclamation. But the Fifty-fourth's actions in battle would soon prove that its soldiers were more than symbols, catapulting Shaw's company to the status of legend.

The call came on July 16, when the regiment was still recovering from its first action in South Carolina. Their next assignment, handed down by General Quincy A. Gillmore, was to march to Morris Island, where they would support an infantry assault on Charleston's Fort Wagner. Wagner was the last defense between the Union and Fort Sumter, where the Confederate rebellion had begun. When Shaw and his weary soldiers reported to General C. Strong the following evening, he offered them a chance to lead the charge against Fort Wagner—an assignment that, if successful, would change the course of the entire war.

Though Shaw knew the risks of the mission and suspected he would die in accepting it, he also sensed that the regiment had been created for just such an act of noble self-sacrifice. At dusk, he led his men to the front and instructed them to "take the fort or die there." After an interval of bombardment, he urged them forward, marching in the lead as they fell "like grass before a sickle." Barraged by the batteries of both Wagner and Sumter, the Fifty-fourth never flinched as its surviving members scaled the sloping sand walls of the fort. Only a few remained with Shaw when he made his last stand on the parapet, waving his sword in defiance as an enemy bullet took his life.

The men fought on without their commander after his body had fallen into the fort, withdrawing only after a full hour on the embattled wall. Of the eight hundred Union soldiers that died that day, more than a quarter were African Americans—twenty of whom were thrown into an unmarked grave with Shaw on the orders of a Confederate general. The Confederates intended the mass grave as a blow to the concept of whites leading blacks into battle, informing Shaw's father, "We buried him with his niggers." Instead, the mingling of the aristocratic colonel and the black men who died with him served as a symbol for brotherhood between black and white. The grave's importance was underlined when Shaw's parents refused to have their son exhumed and returned to Boston, writing that they could think of "no holier place" for him to lie than among "his brave and devoted soldiers."

This regiment is preserved at the peak of "hope and glory" in Augustus Saint-Gaudens's famous memorial on Boston Common, which captures Shaw and his men marching toward battle in seamless solidarity. Regarded as one of America's most powerful pieces of public sculpture, the bronze relief embodies the moral awakening inspired by the Fifty-fourth. Here, as in life, are the men who marched past the State House that cloudless spring day, inspiring one incredulous reporter to write, "Is this Boston? Is this America?"

THE INVENTION OF THE TELEPHONE

- 1876 -

SLEEP DEPRIVED AND ABSENTMINDED, Alexander Graham Bell settled in for another all-nighter in the lab, accompanied by his assistant, Thomas A. Watson. Watson was on a different floor as Bell moved toward the primitive receiver he'd designed to test his theory. Before he got there, he knocked over a container of sulfuric acid they'd been using as a conducting liquid, soaking a perfectly good pair of pants in the process. "Mr. Watson, come here, I want you," he blurted into the mouthpiece, little thinking that, with these words, he had launched a new era in communications.

Bell had every reason to be distracted as he puttered around his laboratory the evening of March 10, 1876. Taking a sabbatical from his position at Boston University had been risky enough for the impoverished professor, but he'd further jeopardized his stability by going against the express wishes of his benefactors. These patrons had insisted that he limit his experiments to the project he'd initially pitched to them: the creation of a "harmonic telegraph" that could send multiple messages simultaneously, over the same wire. It was this innovation that held the most promise, they assured him, not his self-indulgent experiments with electric speech transmission.

If his benefactors had been in control only of his funding, Bell might have felt more confident in moonlighting on his "scientific toy." But one of the men also had the power to determine his future happiness, for he was the father of Mabel Hubbard, a former student Bell hoped to marry. Though generous with his support and vocal with his encouragement, Gardiner G. Hubbard had made Mabel's hand a condition of their agreement. "If you wish my daughter," he had told the crestfallen Bell, "you must abandon your foolish telephone."

All such considerations fell by the wayside when Watson appeared at Bell's side, no longer exhausted despite the grueling hours they'd been working. "I can hear you!" he shouted in his partner's face. "I can hear the *words!*" The latter distinction was important after months of experimentation with the device, which had so far yielded plenty of sounds but no intelligible speech.

Armed with proof that the "toy" could transmit conversations through walls and across space, Bell was able to convince Mr. Hubbard that his project was more than a pipe dream. Hubbard and Bell's other backer, Thomas Sanders, were compensated for their ongoing investment by becoming partners in the fledgling Bell Company, which held a monopoly on the manufacture of telephones for the next nineteen years.

Before his immersion in the field of electric communications, Bell had been equally obsessed with teaching the deaf to speak. The son of a deaf mother and Alexander Melville, a second-generation expert in elocution, Bell initially came to Boston to teach his father's pioneering system of "Visible Speech," a method of showing the deaf how to vocalize by coaching them in the positioning of the lips, tongue, and throat. It was in this capacity, as head of his own School of Vocal Physiology, that he met Mabel Hubbard, who'd been rendered deaf and mute by a childhood attack of scarlet fever.

Had Bell not been driven by the desire to improve the lives of his mother and future wife, he may never have become so fixated on the telephone. His work on electric speech transmission was an outgrowth of previous experiments for the deaf—among them the attempt to create an alphabet of vibrations, so that deaf mutes could be taught to master speech through sight. In pursuit of this goal, he once used a severed ear from a human cadaver as a transmitter, observing of the eardrum, "If this tiny disc can vibrate a bone, then an iron disc might vibrate an iron rod, or at least, an iron wire."

The same logic would surface in his initial technology for the telephone, which consisted of little more than a couple of receivers, a wire, and an electric current supplied by two magnets. As rudimentary as this device must have seemed, its ability to transmit sounds was compelling enough to secure Bell a patent. Patent 174,465, which was secured on March 7 (the inventor's twenty-ninth birthday), remains "the most valuable single patent ever issued" in any country, eventually making millionaires of Bell and his loyal supporters.

But before it became a household necessity, the telephone had to make its public debut. Its unveiling was scheduled for the 1876 Centennial Exposition in Philadelphia, where it would be included in an exhibit at the Department of Education. By the time this plan was decided, Bell had resumed his professorial duties for lack of any other source of income. He was far too broke to accompany his invention to Philadelphia and expected the Hubbards to attend in his stead.

His plans changed when he went to help Mabel board the train for Philadelphia, at which point she learned that he was staying behind. As Bell watched longingly from the platform, his bride-to-be begged him to come with her, eventually dissolving in tears as the train steamed out of the station. The sight of Mabel in distress was too much for the smitten inventor, who forgot his commitments in Boston and sprinted to catch the moving train. His behavior may have seemed irrational to those who watched him drag his six-foot frame onto the caboose, but it would have made perfect sense to his assistant. Having observed Bell over months of intense collaboration, Watson said: "I never saw a man so much in love as Bell was."

Though the exposition was a resounding success, marked by raves from notable figures including the emperor of Brazil (who exclaimed, "My God! It talks!"), Bell would not have long to bask in his achievements. Over the next eleven years, his telephone patent would be dogged by six hundred legal challenges, the most convincing from an inventor named Elisha Gray.

Gray had been breathing down Bell's neck in the race to invent the harmonic telegraph, and on the very day the application for Patent 174,465 was filed, he had filed his own "caveat" for an instrument capable of wiring speech. Despite a lifetime of progressively more hostile attempts to claim ownership of the telephone, Gray couldn't change the fact that a caveat expressed the *intent* to invent, while a patent application presented the invention as a fait accompli. Even without this technicality—and the fact that the theory outlined in his caveat failed to produce a working telephone—Gray would have remained in Bell's wake. For not only had Bell "discovered a new art—that of transmitting speech by electricity," but his had been the fifth claim into the patent office on a day when Gray's was the thirty-ninth.

It took another 599 lawsuits for imposters to tire of contesting Bell's patent. His status as inventor was upheld in every instance, and the value of his company's stock rose with each significant victory. By the time Bell and Mabel exchanged vows in the summer of 1877, it was clear that a stake in Bell Telephone would be valuable. Bell himself certainly knew this when he presented her with his version of a wedding dowry: all but ten of the shares he'd collected as inventor, which amounted to a full third of the newly formed company.

Both the status of his invention and his future with Mabel hung in the balance the night the telephone spoke its first words, leaving Bell in a state of limbo with little to lean on but Watson. By the time the sun rose over their Exeter Place laboratory the next day, both men must have suspected the impact their work would have on future generations. In the words of Thomas Edison, who had tried and failed to invent the telephone before Bell, their device had done nothing less than "[annihilate] time and space . . . and [bring] the human family closer in touch."

THE *TITANIC* OF NEW ENGLAND

- 1898 -

THE WIND HAD BEEN STRENGTHENING ALL EVENING when the passengers began to board the coastal steamer *Portland,* anticipating a routine overnight journey to Portland, Maine. It was the night before Thanksgiving, and the 290-foot paddle-wheel steamer was filled to capacity for the trip up the coast. If the 192 passengers noticed the thickening cloud cover as they departed Boston's India Wharf, it would scarcely have been cause for concern. Anyone familiar with Boston Novembers would have seen his fair share of nor'easters, and most native New Englanders would have considered it bad form to overreact about the weather.

When the *Portland* left shore at 7:00 that night, her captain (Hollis Blanchard) and owners (the Portland Steam Packet Company) were aware that a storm was heading north from the Gulf of Mexico, as its winds had been tossing the seas off New York throughout the day. The forecast was dire enough to make them cancel the evening voyage of *Portland's* sister ship, the *Bay State,* which was scheduled to leave Portland for Boston at the same time, but Blanchard must have been confident that he could reach Maine before the winds caught up with him.

Unfortunately, this plan had a major blind spot—one that was shared by hundreds of people who braved coastal waters that evening. A second low-pressure zone was building over the Great Lakes as the *Portland* ferried its passengers home for the holidays, and the collision of both fronts would lead to the most destructive gale the region had ever seen.

The first sign that something was amiss came forty minutes into the journey, when snow began to fall and rapidly escalated into a blizzard. Unaware that the southern storm would soon merge with hurricane-force winds from the north, Blanchard may have felt it wiser to continue on rather then return to Boston. The two storms became one sometime between 9:30 and 11:00 P.M., at which point it was too late for the *Portland* to seek harbor. As winds increased from forty miles per hour (at 11:00 P.M.) to gusts of up to ninety miles per hour (at 3:00 A.M.), her only choice was to head for open water, where she had a better chance of riding out the storm without shattering.

What little is known of the *Portland's* progress that night comes from the testimony of witnesses onshore. She was spotted off of Thacher Island (only thirty miles north of Boston) at 9:30 P.M., a position that indicates how badly she'd been thwarted by the driving wind. Further sightings were reported between 11:00 and 11:45 P.M., each indicating extreme damage to the hull as the gale drove her southward.

Little more was seen of the *Portland* until morning, though lifesavers on Cape Cod heard a steamer's whistle at 5:45 A.M. Between 9:00 and 10:30 A.M., when the eye of the storm passed over, it is believed that the battered vessel remained floundering within eight miles of shore. By this time, the gravity of the situation had long been apparent to both the passengers and those awaiting them in Portland. Wreckage and bodies from many smaller boats had washed ashore throughout the night, and thousands of sailors remained missing at daybreak.

Onshore, it looked like the aftermath of the apocalypse. In Boston, telegraph lines had been swept away and railroad tracks had been washed out. Whole houses were sheared from their foundations on Cape Cod, some of them floating with the furious tide all the way to the coast of Maine. Further north in Scituate, waves taller than buildings had redesigned the shoreline, carving a new inlet to the North River and depositing enough silt to close its mouth. This alteration would be permanent, partially reversing the river's flow and serving as a living testament to the storm's magnitude.

The gale persisted for three nights, and by the time it exhausted itself on the morning of Tuesday, November 29, more than 450 people had drowned and 141 boats (among them 53 schooners) lay on the ocean floor. The first sign that the *Portland* had not survived came at 7:30 P.M. on Sunday, November 27, little more than twenty-four hours after the pride of the New England steamship fleet departed Boston. A Cape Cod rescue worker was combing the beach for survivors when he came upon a life preserver emblazoned with the *Portland*'s name. Further flotsam was to follow, including several forty-quart dairy cans and doors wrested from the steamer's palatial interior.

All hope of survivors was abandoned by 9:30 P.M., when a ship's worth of wreckage arrived on the rising tide. Only thirty-six bodies were recovered, robbing families of the comfort of burying lost loved ones. More frustrating still was the fact that the only passenger manifest went down with the *Portland*, making it impossible for friends of the missing to be certain they'd made the trip.

Since the last sighting of the distressed boat was between 9:00 and 10:30 A.M. on November 27, and the first bodies were discovered

after 9:30 that night, it is not known how long she was able to with-
stand the waves. The storm whipped up again soon after she was last
spotted, and it's impossible to imagine how harrowing her final hours
must have been for those remaining aboard. The one clue to the time
of her demise can be read two ways, as several of the bodies recovered
wore watches that had stopped at 9:15. Since witnesses were vague
about the exact time they had seen her intact offshore, experts were
unable to ascertain whether she sank in the morning or only
moments before the bulk of her wreckage was found.

Either outcome held little solace for friends and relatives
onshore, who waited eagerly for news of the steamer's fate. But even
this sad closure was delayed by the storm's devastation, which had
grounded the telegraph cables between Cape Cod and Boston.
Reports of the *Portland's* loss eventually reached New England by
way of France and New York, patched through by transatlantic cable
and other undersea networks.

Due to the majesty of the vessel and the magnitude of the loss,
the storm was named after the *Portland,* which henceforth was
known as "the *Titanic* of New England." Though the *Boston Daily
Globe* reported that the steamer had wrecked off of Highland Light,
her whereabouts remained a mystery until 1989, when three members of the Historic Maritime Group of New England (HMGNE)
located a wreck they believed to be the *Portland.* Their suspicions
were conclusively resolved in 2002, when advanced technology
helped them to identify her battered remains and chart her position
on the ocean floor.

But the wreck's location—under three hundred feet of water off
of Cape Ann—wasn't the only revelation yielded by the HMGNE's
wide-scan sonar and remotely operated vehicles. The scan also produced a likely theory for the *Portland's* last moments, thanks to the
discovery of the *Addie E. Snow* less than a quarter mile away. Named

for a girl who turned nineteen the year of the crash, the *Addie E. Snow* was a two-masted schooner from Rockland, Maine. Trapped in the wind tunnel that the Massachusetts Bay must have become during the squall, both vessels had been blown wildly off course: the *Portland* making no headway in its efforts to steam up the coast, the *Addie E. Snow* buffeted leeward at the mercy of conflicting currents.

In the blinding snow that accompanied the storm at its peak, all navigational aids would have been useless to determine location. It's entirely possible that the *Portland,* a towering white vessel with gold trim, was all but invisible to the smaller ship until moments before they collided. Because of its narrowness and disproportionate height, the *Portland* would have capsized easily upon impact, while the *Addie E. Snow* could scarcely have survived the damage of a crash at high speed.

Whether the two ships crossed paths in their final moments or met separate disasters in the same spot, they are united for all eternity in the depths of the North Atlantic. Due to her dramatic fate, the *Portland* would be the last of her breed, as propeller-driven ships began to replace paddle-wheel steamers on the perilous route between Boston and Portland. Her legacy looms large in the maritime lore of New England—and in the protocol of modern-day captains, who never set sail without leaving a passenger list onshore.

HOUDINI JUMPS OFF
THE HARVARD BRIDGE

- 1908 -

IT WAS STANDING ROOM ONLY on the Harvard Bridge that day, and even more onlookers craned their necks from their positions on the bridge's supports. The audience spread along the shore and spilled onto the choppy Charles River, where a flotilla of boats jockeyed for position within view of the spectacle above. All eyes were fixed on the figure of a wild-haired, grim-faced man at the bridge's railing—a man whose unseasonable bathing costume would have seemed bizarre even if it hadn't been accessorized with manacles and heavy chains. The man paced among the wool-suited men and long-skirted women of the crowd, seemingly oblivious to the chill of the April day. No one lifted a finger to stop him when he hoisted himself to the bridge's railing, coiling his wrestler's body for a jump that could scarcely be survived.

A hush fell over the onlookers as the chained man sank to the river's bottom. As seconds passed, nervous chatter erupted, followed by anguished silence. After what seemed like an eternity but was actually only a minute, a sleek head broke the waves in the shadows under the bridge. A cheer came up from surrounding boaters as they saw that the swimmer wore no chains, having somehow unshackled himself on the floor of the frigid Charles. As astonishing as the stunt had been, it was little more than a preview of coming attractions from the man who performed it—a teaser, a taste, a fleeting glimpse of what could happen when Houdini came to town.

As publicity schemes go, the manacled jump was a smashing success, and Houdini drew record crowds for his two-week run at Boston's Keith's Theatre. He was the headliner of a vaudeville act that included the Colonial Septette, Herbert the Frogman, the Outlaw Trio, and an ensemble of Japanese acrobats. In keeping with his image as the master of the "Impossible Possible," the famous escape artist risked his reputation nightly by accepting challenges from the audience. Though this habit caused him few problems while in Boston, he had "one of the closest shaves in his career" on a subsequent trip to Portland, Maine, where a fan locked him into a pair of handcuffs it took thirty minutes to escape from.

A typical Houdini act in 1908 was anything but ordinary. Hailed as the king of vaudeville for his death-defying escapes and extravagant illusions, he earned his crown by keeping his audiences guessing. One night's show might find him immersed in an airtight, galvanized iron can, filled to capacity with water and secured by locks supplied by the audience—only to emerge moments later, dripping wet but otherwise unscathed.

Another showstopper was his famous "hindoo needle trick," wherein he invited the public (and especially the doctors in the house) to come onstage and conduct a close examination of his mouth. This oral exam was a prelude to a peculiar stunt in which he swallowed fifty needles and several yards of thread. After a suitable interlude for digestion, he would then regurgitate the eaten needles, which had somehow become threaded during their journey to his stomach.

With stunts like these up his sleeve, he hardly needed the extra buzz he drew from hurling himself into the Charles River. But such exploits were all in a day's work for a specialist in "impossible" spectacles, and no one who witnessed it would forget the splash Houdini made when he came to Boston.

CURLEY STEALS THE MAYOR'S SEAT

- 1913 -

"TOODLES:" THE REFERENCE WENT OVER THE HEADS of the attendees at his political rallies, but it wasn't the man on the street that James Michael Curley was targeting with this particular message . . . not yet. In a series of campaign speeches leading up to Boston's 1913 mayoral election, Curley had begun announcing his intent to lecture on the topic "Great Lovers in History: From Cleopatra to Toodles." This may have seemed nonsensical to Boston voters but, to incumbent Mayor John F. Fitzgerald, it was a politically charged poison arrow. On December 18 Fitzgerald announced that he was withdrawing from the race on the advice of his doctor. Having dispatched with his most imposing obstacle, Curley went on to win by a sizable margin, launching the first of what would eventually amount to four terms as mayor.

Fitzgerald was one of countless statesmen who would be trampled in Curley's climb to power, having initially had the audacity to defend his seat rather than stepping aside for the younger Irish

Democrat. Having expected Fitzgerald to run for the Senate, Curley viewed his presence in the mayoral contest as a betrayal. His revenge for this perceived slight arrived at Fitzgerald's house in the form of a black-bordered letter addressed to the mayor's wife, Josephine. In this letter, Mrs. Fitzgerald was spared no detail of her husband's liaison with a twenty-three-year-old cigarette girl named "Toodles," with whom he'd been seen cavorting at a suburban roadhouse near Boston. As if knowledge of the affair weren't bad enough, the letter threatened to expose it to the public unless the mayor withdrew immediately from the race. Curley followed up with periodic mentions of "Toodles" on the campaign trail, leaving Fitzgerald little choice but to comply with the terms of the blackmail or risk bringing disgrace on his wife and children.

Over the course of more than half a century, Curley's name would become synonymous with Boston politics, surfacing in thirty-two election campaigns for a variety of offices including the common council, state representative, alderman, U.S. Congress, governor, and U.S. Senate. Each of these campaigns was marked by strategies similar to the one he used against Fitzgerald. "Politics and holiness are not always synonymous," he once said, in a rare instance of understatement. "There are times . . . when, if you wish to win an election, you must do unto others as they wish they could do unto you, but you must do it first."

Curley's political headquarters was called the Tammany Club and its symbol was a crouching tiger. In keeping with this predatory theme, Curley sharpened his claws on opposing candidates in each successive election, often exploiting the resentments of his fellow Boston Irish. This habit was a departure from the prevailing tradition of local politics, in which ethnic and religious considerations remained largely unspoken. Turn-of-the-century Mayor Patrick Collins (1901–1905), who had previously served as the first Irishman ever elected to the Massachusetts State Senate, was typical of this kinder, gentler climate on Beacon Hill.

Collins saw only rancor in the divisive tactics Curley later made popular. "Let me say that there are no Irish voters among us," he said in a speech that found favor with constituents in 1876. "There are Irish-born citizens . . . but the moment the seal of the court was impressed on our papers we ceased to be foreigners and became Americans."

To Curley such conciliatory statements were in direct conflict with the actual experience of Irish immigrants, who were a despised and persecuted minority in Boston until they became—to the chagrin of the Yankee Protestants who had always ruled the city—the majority. A perceptive and ruthless strategist, he saw the avoidance of ethnic issues as a missed opportunity.

Decades of inequality had imbued the Boston Irish with an understandable "us versus them" mentality, and Curley was among the first Irish leaders to realize the political pay dirt in channeling this anger. This tactic, however, was ineffectual in contests with fellow Irishmen, and this was the predicament Curley faced in his campaign against Mayor Fitzgerald. Unlike future opponents such as Joseph Ely (whom Curley accused of "vicious and contemptible hatred for the Irish race") and Thomas Hopkinson Eliot (whose Unitarian faith he lampooned as that "unfortunate denomination"), Fitzgerald could not be linked to a Puritan pedigree or inflammatory remarks against the Irish.

With his initial mayoral election in 1905, Fitzgerald had become the nation's first American-born Irish-Catholic mayor. On the campaign trail, he was not above playing the race card, at one point promoting himself in a political ad that pitted "Manhood" (as represented by a photograph of himself and his six children) against "Money" (as personified by James Jackson Storrow, his blue-blooded opponent). But despite his marital indiscretions, he was a moral paragon compared to Curley, who had conducted his 1903 campaign for alderman from the confines of the Charles Street Jail.

One of his first successes, Curley's jailhouse win announced the arrival of a politician with the nerve to try anything and the charisma to pull it off. If a stunt worked once, he tried it twice, and this technique even applied to combining politics and prison, which he did again during his fourth and final term as mayor in 1947. Both convictions were for fraud, with the first occurring when he and a colleague took the civil service examination—and cheated on it—on behalf of two illiterate Irish friends. His second arrest was for his affiliation with an organization called the Engineers' Group, Inc.—a conflict of interest because the group's stated purpose was to procure government contracts for small businesses. Since this setup placed Curley, as a government official, in a position to award contracts to his own clients for a percentage of the profits, this was a violation of his oath of office. And, since the majority of businesses that paid the Engineers' Group for its connections had not received a single contract in return, the scheme would have been a fraud even without the potential for kickbacks to Curley.

It should have served as a handicap, but Curley's popularity was such that his imprisonment only added to his mystique. Rather than ignoring his first jail term as most candidates would, he incorporated it into his campaign platform, adopting the slogan, "He did it for a friend." Having seen Curley commit political suicide and survive, Mayor Fitzgerald had little hope of emerging on top in 1913. Two days after his wife received the blackmail letter, he injured himself in a fall down a flight of stairs while inspecting a decrepit boardinghouse. Though the other opposing candidates suspended their campaigns while he was recovering, Curley stepped up his schedule of public appearances, going so far as to schedule a rally at a school on Fitzgerald's street.

So it was that a bedridden Fitzgerald was subjected to Curley's shouted taunts from beyond his window. Far from softening his blows out of sympathy for the mayor's condition, Curley continued his attack, exhorting Fitzgerald to "Get your slippers and pipe and stretch out in your hammock and read *Ladies' Home Journal.*" Exhausted by the ongoing character assassination and ashamed of his exploits with Toodles, Fitzgerald did what Curley had wanted him to do all along. He got out of his way, never to be elected to public office again.

Ironically, Curley's reign—and his life—would come to a close just as the star of Fitzgerald's grandson, John F. Kennedy Jr., was rising. Unlike Curley and Fitzgerald, Kennedy would transcend the infighting of Massachusetts politics to become America's first Irish Catholic president. During his inauguration on January 20, 1961, he was sworn in using Fitzgerald's Bible, giving his dead grandfather a turn on the national stage that Curley (also dead) had always coveted.

Curley's immortality was less dynastic in nature—it came when an author named Edwin O'Connor recognized his life story for the ripping yarn it was and fictionalized it in a novel called *The Last Hurrah.* A best seller, the book was later made into a film starring Spencer Tracy as Frank Skeffington, Curley's alter ego. As flattering as the portrait of Skeffington was on both page and screen, Curley threatened to sue for libel. People outside of Massachusetts may have seen this as a sincere reaction to a breach of privacy, but his former constituents knew what was really happening. Just as he'd done with the Engineers' Group and in a thousand other cons, Curley was using his position to prevent others from profiting until he got his cut of the action.

THE GREAT MOLASSES FLOOD

- 1919 -

GIUSEPPE IANTOSCA WAS STATIONED AT the second-floor window of his home overlooking Commercial Street, watching protectively over his son Pasquale, who was collecting firewood below. Accompanied by his friends, Maria and Antonio Distasio, Pasquale made an afternoon ritual of visiting the harbor-front molasses tank, where both kindling and escaped molasses could be found in abundance. Complicating today's mission was the presence of a Bay State Railroad worker, who was chiding Maria for trespassing while Pasquale and Antonio huddled in the shadows of the fifty-foot tank. With the suddenness that so often separates the ordinary from the unspeakable, the railway worker and all three children were erased from the landscape, swallowed by a tidal wave of molasses traveling at an estimated thirty-five miles per hour.

Iantosca scarcely had time to absorb the horror of what he'd seen before he was thrown back from the window by the force of the molasses explosion. When he regained consciousness, his whole neighborhood was afloat in a sticky deluge that would claim twenty-one lives—among them the lives of Maria and Pasquale, who had been standing directly in the path of the crushing wave when the tank gave way. Miraculously, Antonio survived with a fractured skull and a concussion, having been plucked from the molasses by a firefighter after the blast hurled him headfirst into a lamppost.

What happens when a steel tank filled with 2.3 million gallons of molasses erupts in a densely populated neighborhood? In breathless reports of the disaster, the *Boston Globe* itemized the extremity of the damages: "Fragments of the great tank were thrown up into the air, buildings in the neighborhood began to crumble up as though the underpinnings had been pulled away from them, and scores of people in the various buildings were buried in the ruins, some dead and others badly injured." A large shard of the tank smashed into a trestle supporting the elevated train track, buckling the structure moments after the passage of a northbound train. A brakeman named Royal Albert Leeman was able to warn off the conductor of a second train as it approached from North Station, bringing it to a screeching halt just in time to prevent it from plunging off the broken track to Commercial Street.

Centered in the sights of the explosion was the Engine 31 firehouse, where firefighters were whiling away their lunch hour with a game of whist when the wave swept the building from its foundation. The impact of the molasses, traveling faster than a fire engine at full throttle, pounded the second story of the three-floor building into the first, trapping the unsuspecting card players in an eighteen-inch crawl space. Though some of the firefighters survived the collapse with substantial injuries, an eight-year veteran named George Layhe was unable to hold his head above the rising tide of molasses that swirled around him. Layhe drowned only moments before rescue workers reached him by cutting through the floor above. He was discovered under the splintered remains of a pool table and a piano.

As the death toll was tallied and area hospitals were overwhelmed by the injured, the tank's owners were already formulating their defense strategy. Playing on the widespread phobia of anarchists and other anti-American agitators, U.S. Industrial Alcohol (USIA) dispatched its attorney to the scene to read a statement suggesting that "outside influences" had caused the tank to explode. This claim ran counter to the evidence available to North End residents, most of whom had noticed the tank leaking since its completion in January 1916. Indeed, molasses seeped from its seams in such copious amounts that neighborhood children salvaged it in buckets—a habit that had entertained Pasquale Iantosca and his friends in happier days.

The structure's instability was the result of its hasty construction; the tank's completion had been rushed to accommodate America's increasing demand for industrial alcohol. Distilled from molasses, industrial alcohol was an important ingredient in the manufacture of munitions, and the demand for munitions had been on the rise ever since the beginning of World War I. Though President Woodrow Wilson had initially vowed to preserve America's neutrality, the escalating aggression of the Germans would eventually provoke him to join the war. Once America added its troops to the Allied Forces, munitions manufacture assumed the status of a patriotic duty, ensuring that business would be booming for USIA until an armistice was reached.

As one of the country's leading producers of industrial alcohol, USIA had increased its net profits nearly ninefold between 1914 and 1916. The hasty completion of the Boston tank would pave the way for more of the same, freeing the company from reliance on third-party suppliers and storage facilities. Looming on the horizon was the imminent arrival of a tanker from the Cuba Distilling Company, which would unload its seven hundred thousand gallons of molasses elsewhere if USIA couldn't accommodate them. Faced with this deadline, USIA Treasurer Arthur P. Jell exhorted the owners of Hammond Iron Works to work fast, forgoing the recommended safety test (which required that the tank be filled to capacity with water) in favor of a cursory inspection (using only six inches of water).

Over the ensuing months, North Enders grew familiar with the sight of molasses dripping sloppily down the sides of the mammoth tank, and some even heard it emit rumbling sounds similar to thunder. Because molasses is a substance prone to fermentation (the process by which sugar is transformed into alcohol), and fermentation is a process that produces carbon dioxide, it is likely that the expansion of this gas exerted pressure on the sides of the tank whenever it was full.

Though the tank's constant leakage must have inspired doubts about its structural integrity, USIA's only response to these doubts was to have the tank caulked (thereby sealing the seams and perhaps increasing the internal pressure). They also made the disingenuous decision to paint the tank a muddy brown color, matching it to the molasses so the seepage would be harder to see.

In the aftermath of the tragedy, 119 separate legal claims were levied against USIA by bereaved and injured victims of the molasses flood. The property damage on the waterfront was estimated at more than one million dollars, a staggering sum for the time. The Massachusetts Superior Court ruled that the separate claims should be consolidated into a single trial, and USIA's defense was led by Charles Choate, while Damon Everett Hall argued for the plaintiffs. The esteemed Colonel Hugh W. Ogden was assigned the role of "auditor" for the trial, forming opinions on liability and potential damages after each side submitted its evidence.

As expected, Choate's strategy was to absolve the company of all blame, insisting that "evilly disposed persons" had sabotaged the tank in broad daylight. He called on an assortment of expert witnesses to support this claim, capitalizing on the rampant fear of radicals, Communists, and anarchists that were afoot at the time. Hall scoffed at the idea of a "mythical bomb," focusing instead on the very real loss of life, livelihood, and property that followed the explosion. He also presented exhaustive evidence of the tank's flawed construction, condemning USIA for gross negligence and "an absolute and utter disregard of the rights of the public, of the people in the houses and buildings adjacent to where this structure was erected."

Had Ogden judged in favor of the defense (Choate and USIA), victims like Giuseppe Iantosca would receive no compensation for the loss of their loved ones. The wave that destroyed a neighborhood within seconds would be chalked up to the actions of invisible evildoers, giving USIA carte blanche to rush construction of a tank in some other community. To some, this outcome seemed inevitable, since Colonel Ogden had far more in common with the capitalists who had built the tank than the working-class immigrants who had suffered from it.

With such preconceptions in place, it came as a surprise when Ogden issued a verdict supporting the plaintiffs, recommending that they be reimbursed to the tune of $300,000 (comparable to $3 million today). Hall eventually negotiated for a settlement of $628,000, which USIA agreed to pay rather than risk the expense of a jury trial.

Though any amount of money would seem modest in comparison with the losses endured by the neighborhood, the trial's benefits were more than purely monetary. Having seen that justice was not the property of business owners and Brahmins, many of Boston's apolitical immigrants chose to engage in the community by becoming citizens. Whereas many immigrants—and Italians in particular—had previously remained aloof from the political process, spending their lives in America without ever voting or applying for citizenship, the molasses disaster ushered in a citizenship boom in Boston and beyond.

In addition to inspiring many immigrants to claim their voices as Americans, the molasses trial gave rise to stricter safety standards for big businesses. In a move that was echoed around the country, the Boston Building Department instituted new laws for engineering certification, requiring engineers and architects to submit their calculations and signed drawings to the city. Improved regulations also made it impossible for companies to get a building permit without a seal of approval from a registered engineer—a bit of red tape that might have saved twenty-one lives and untold heartache had it been passed before the construction of the North End molasses tank.

THE FATEFUL SALE OF BABE RUTH

- 1919 -

Harry Frazee had always said that the best thing about Boston was the train to New York. Since buying the Boston Red Sox in 1917, the absentee owner had split his attention between Fenway Park and the footlights of Broadway, where he was a theater owner and producer of frothy fare such as *Nothing but the Truth, Madame Sherry,* and *Leave It to Jane.* Despite a willingness to spend and a promise to deliver "a first-class article" to Red Sox fans, Frazee's biggest asset remained a player who'd been signed before his time: a left-handed pitcher named George Herman Ruth, whose batting average (.300, with eleven homers and sixty-four RBIs) topped the American League in 1918.

During Ruth's tenure in Boston, the Red Sox won the World Series three times, sealing their status as the most successful franchise in major league baseball. This same era found the New York Yankees floundering at the bottom of the National League, having failed to win so much as a division title since their inception (as the Baltimore

Orioles) in 1901. Little did Boston's rabid fans know that these roles would soon be reversed, leaving their team under a cloud that would come to be known as the "Curse of the Bambino."

The fateful deal was done in New York, but its fallout would be felt in Boston throughout the remainder of the twentieth century. Knowing that Frazee's revenues (both in the box office and the ball-park) had dwindled due to World War I and recognizing Ruth as his most valuable commodity, Yankees owners Colonel Huston and Jacob Ruppert made him an offer he couldn't ignore: $100,000 and a loan of $350,000, which he could use to purchase Fenway Park from its previous owners. When the agreement was finalized on December 26, 1919, the bill of sale for Ruth alone was $125,000. It was the highest sum that had ever been paid for a baseball player, and not a person in either city would deny it was a bargain.

To hear Frazee tell it, he had no choice. History has canonized Ruth as the greatest hitter that ever lived, but at the time he was a thorn in the side of the cash-strapped owner. Temperamental, cocky, and incapable of keeping a curfew, he was larger than life and expected to be paid that way. Despite having agreed to a three-year contract for ten thousand dollars per year, he'd taken stock of his status on the team and was now threatening to hold out if he didn't get twenty thousand dollars in 1920.

True to his name, the Bambino was prone to throwing tantrums when he didn't get his way and had once deserted the Red Sox (and signed, for a brief time, with a team in the Delaware River Ship-building League) after being fined for screaming at his manager. When negotiations began between Frazee, Ruppert, and Huston, Babe Ruth was on a barnstorming tour of the West Coast, where he endeared himself to no one by attacking the weather and expressing an interest in the movies—an interest he'd pursue, he told reporters, for a fee of no less than ten thousand dollars just to show up. His image has been airbrushed over the intervening decades, but the media of his day accused him of being selfish, petulant, and toxic to the morale of other players . . . exactly the kind of adjectives applied to contemporary divas like Terrell Owens.

Frazee emphasized the star's dark side in his statement to the media on January 5, 1920, a day Red Sox fans would remember as Black Monday. In a statement that seems laughable in hindsight, the owner suggested that the Yankees were "taking a gamble" on the volatile Bambino, who "had no regard for the feelings of anyone but himself." Citing two instances in which Ruth had "jumped the club and revolted," Frazee justified the sale by railing against the drawbacks of a "one-man club."

History would prove that if the Yankees were gambling, they were doing so with a stacked deck. Anchored by the power hitting of Ruth, they would win their first American League pennant in 1921, getting their first taste of a winning streak that would yield six pennants and three World Series championships in the 1920s alone. As for the "Olde Towne Team," it would morph from a successful "one-man club" to a hapless no-man's-land, as Frazee paid his debt to Ruppert by sending players like "Sad" Sam Jones, "Jumpin'" Joe Dugan, Herb Pennock, Deacon Everett Scott, "Bullet" Joe Bush, and Waite Hoyt to New York.

In Ruth's absence, the Red Sox rapidly unraveled, spending the next decade in the basement of the American League and racking up losing seasons between 1920 and 1934. Some inkling of this impending disaster was felt in the aftermath of Frazee's announcement, when one Boston paper published a cartoon depicting FOR SALE signs on other local institutions—among them Boston Common, Faneuil Hall, and Paul Revere's statue. Nick Flatley of the *Boston Evening American* echoed the sentiments of many when he wrote that in dealing Ruth, "a bird that hops into the picture once in a lifetime," the Red Sox had "lost the greatest drawing card the game has ever known."

In light of the outcome, it's easy to regard Frazee as the ultimate Judas, knowingly pawning Boston's future for his own gain. But Boston's dominance was already endangered by a number of factors in 1919—among them flagging attendance at games due to the war, which left Frazee struggling to pay the salaries of his marquee players. Adding to his instability was the fact that he was little more than a tenant at Fenway Park, renting it from a realty trust controlled by former Red Sox owners Charles Taylor and Joseph Lannin.

Not holding the deed to the stadium gave Frazee a tenuous hold on the team itself—a situation that became urgent once he found himself in a feud with American League President Ban Johnson. Johnson had long nursed a grudge against Frazee, seeing him as an interloper whose talents were better suited to show business than baseball. He seized the chance to act on this grudge when the Red Sox sold a star pitcher named Carl Mays to the Yankees. What made the deal controversial was the fact that Johnson had recommended suspension for Mays, who had violated league rules by abandoning the club in midseason. But Mays was worth nothing to Frazee on suspension, and the Yankees were willing to buy him for seventy-five thousand dollars and two lesser-known pitchers (Allen Russell and Bob McGraw).

Johnson was livid about the transaction and ordered the Yankees to observe Mays's suspension before playing him. The Yankees upped the ante by taking the matter to court, and the ensuing battle split the American League into two opposing parties: the "Insurrectos," a group comprised of the Red Sox, the Yankees, and the Chicago White Sox; and the "Loyal Five," which consisted of everyone else. The battle came to a boil in the autumn of 1919, with Johnson threatening to revoke the Red Sox franchise and rescind Frazee's rights as an owner.

When Frazee later spoke about the deed that would follow him to his grave, he said, "the Ruth deal was the only way I could retain the Red Sox." With no claim on Fenway Park and mounting legal debts to pay, he had little hope of holding on to the team if Johnson followed through on his threats. The feud with Johnson made it imperative that Frazee find a way to buy Fenway. If he didn't, another owner could take over simply by purchasing a lease on the stadium.

These particulars are rarely mentioned in the lore surrounding the so-called curse, which generally suggests that Frazee sold Ruth to finance a Broadway production of *No, No, Nanette*. In fact, *No, No, Nanette* never saw the stage until two years after Frazee sold the Red Sox (five years after the sale of Ruth), so its cost is unlikely to have been a factor in the fateful decision.

Whatever his reasons, Frazee will never be redeemed in the eyes of Red Sox fans. Even if keeping Ruth meant losing the Fenway, the franchise, and every other viable player in the dugout, he will always be blamed for bringing bad luck to a team that had formerly seemed blessed. As for Ruth, he never admitted to placing a hex on the club that sold him, eventually returning to Boston for a stint with the Braves (the city's other baseball team) before retiring in 1935.

Until the curse was reversed in 2004, the main evidence of its existence lay in Boston's penchant for spectacular losses—losses that were inevitably snatched from the jaws of victory. Whether its outcome was a curse or a fluke, the facts of Ruth's sale can scarcely be denied: While Yankee Stadium became "The House That Ruth Built," witnessing twenty-six World Series victories between 1920 and 2004, the Red Sox launched one of the longest championship droughts in sports history, making it back to the World Series four times (1946, 1967, 1975, and 1986), but always losing in seven games.

THE RISE AND FALL
OF CHARLES PONZI

- 1921 -

UNITED STATES DISTRICT ATTORNEY Daniel J. Gallagher could scarcely contain his glee when Charles Ponzi entered his Devonshire Street office, his trademark walking stick over his arm and his attorney, Dan Coakley, at his side. Any doubt Gallagher may have had about the purpose of the visit was erased by Ponzi's uncharacteristically sober attire. After a summer of wearing white suits and straw boaters, the diminutive financier was dressed in keeping with the clouds that now followed him—in dark gray, with a chalk stripe and a tie bland enough for a banker.

If Gallagher expected an admission of wrongdoing, he had underestimated Ponzi's capacity for self-delusion. The wily millionaire may have come to turn himself in, but he did not consider a confession to be part of the bargain. Despite the fact that the morning papers had printed mug shots from a previous arrest (Ponzi had been imprisoned twice before: in Montreal for forgery and in Atlanta for smuggling illegal aliens), he did not see himself as a criminal. Even as Gallagher led him to the office of U.S. Marshal Patrick J. Duane to surrender, he was plotting his next comeback.

It had taken investigations at the state and federal level to strip Ponzi of his "million-dollar smile." The so-called wizard of finance had maintained his moxie despite accusations, lawsuits, newspaper exposés, and an exhaustive audit of his holdings in the Securities Exchange Company. But his princely persona concealed the panic of a man who'd been a pauper for most of his life—a status he'd escaped by hatching a scheme that had earned him approximately $9.5 million in seven months.

Ponzi's road to riches—and subsequent ruin—started when he received a letter from Spain. Engaged in an ill-fated import-export venture at the time, he had aspired to publish an international trade magazine titled the *Trader's Guide*. The magazine never materialized, but word of its failure never reached Spain, where a potential subscriber sent for a copy. For postage, he enclosed an International Reply Coupon—a kind of postal currency that could be redeemed for stamps in any post office belonging to the Universal Postal Union.

To the average person, this strange document would scarcely have seemed worth the paper it was printed on. But to Ponzi, it looked like a winning lottery ticket. As was his practice when seized by a vision of dancing dollar signs, he grabbed a piece of paper and began calculating the possibilities.

In a formula almost too complicated to outline, Ponzi hoped to capitalize on struggling world currencies by buying up International Reply Coupons in depressed countries, then redeeming them—first for stamps, then for cash—in America. Since the coupons held a fixed value from one nation to another, he believed he could make exorbitant profits by buying them in his native Italy, where World War I had reduced the lira to an exchange rate of twenty to a dollar.

In his own words, the scheme was no less than a formula for minting money. "The coupon in Spain cost the equivalent of about one cent in American money," he once said of the epiphany that gave rise to his fortune. "I got six cents in stamps for the coupon here. Then I investigated the rates of exchange in other countries. I tried in a small way first. It worked. The first month $1,000 became $15,000. I began letting in my friends. First I accepted deposits on my note, payable in ninety days, for $150 for each $100 received. Though promised in ninety days, I have been paying in forty-five days."

A 50 percent return on any investment . . . an impressive rate of return, if only it had been true. Unfortunately, Ponzi's account was all fiction after his investigation of foreign exchange rates. Blinded by the zeroes his plan could ostensibly add to his bank account, he began advertising for investors before he bothered to test his theory. By the time he discovered, in March 1919, that it was impossible to redeem International Reply Coupons for currency, he had already become the toast of a miracle-starved town, offering 50 percent interest on short-term investments as founder of the Securities Exchange Company.

Never one to be bothered by the fine print, Ponzi began reimbursing his initial investors with the cash invested by new clients. While casting about for some legitimate means of doubling the money he collected, he resorted to the oldest swindle in economic history: the trick of "robbing Peter to pay Paul." Word spread quickly as the first "Ponzi notes" yielded their promised returns, inspiring many to reinvest while telling friends about the easy money they'd made.

Unlike other large-scale fraud schemes, Ponzi's had the benefit of a viable-sounding business model, which he used to convince more skeptical patrons to part with their money. He also had the swagger of a man much larger than his slender five-feet-two-inch frame, and a surplus of charisma that sustained others' belief in him long after the signs of his guilt had surfaced.

In fact, aside from his penchant for pocketing others' savings and his tendency to scoff at the law, Ponzi was exactly the amiable dreamer he pretended to be. He was a devoted husband to his wife, Rose, and genuinely aspired to the role of a modern-day Midas, capable of dispensing wealth to fellow immigrants, strivers, and anyone else who wanted to earn a buck without the inconvenience of working for it.

It was this strange mix of sincerity and duplicity that made Ponzi more than just a typical grifter. As the *New York Times* wrote after his downfall, "there was something picturesque, something suggestive of the gallant about him, and it is almost possible, though not quite, to believe that he was as credulous as his victims and deceived himself as much as he did them."

Ponzi's star reached its zenith on July 24, 1920, when a front-page story in the *Boston Post* catalogued his claims of exorbitant profits under the headline, "DOUBLES THE MONEY WITHIN THREE MONTHS." The article inspired such a rush that Ponzi's chauffeur could scarcely navigate around the crowds on School Street, where the modest Niles Building housed the offices of the Security Exchange Company. When the financier emerged from his lavish blue Locomobile (the most expensive car in America at the time, for which he'd paid $13,600 three weeks earlier), he was surrounded by well-wishers and aspiring investors. When a lone heckler yelled, "I'd like to see the man who could do it," he wasted no time in responding, "Well, I'm doing it! I'm the man!"

Promising as his fortunes looked at the time, Ponzi had less than a month left to enjoy being "the man." Thanks to an audit he himself had requested, in the foolhardy belief that he could create the illusion of cash he'd never had, he would wake to a far different headline on August 12: "ARREST IN PONZI CASE MAY BE MADE TODAY."

It was a coup of some magnitude for Gallagher when Ponzi

surrendered in his office, since state and federal authorities had been angling for the honor of arresting him all summer. Instrumental in establishing his guilt were the inquiries of Bank Commissioner Joseph Allen, who had been observing Ponzi's wildly fluctuating accounts at the Hanover Trust Company. When it became clear that Ponzi's insolvency was on the verge of overdrawing the bank and robbing innocent depositors of their savings, Allen posted a notice ordering Hanover to close its doors pending further investigation.

Unfortunately, Ponzi's liabilities loomed larger than the holdings of one bank, and his arrest touched off one of the worst banking crises in Massachusetts's history. Though the smiling con man cannot be fully blamed for the fallout, the revelation of his guilt was followed by the collapse of four separate banks where he'd kept his money. As for his investors, those who didn't collect their profits in the beginning were reimbursed to the tune of 37.5 percent of their money—a far cry from the 150 percent returns they'd been promised. It took the state's most massive and convoluted bankruptcy hearing to unravel the fine points of Ponzi's financial mismanagement, while the perpetrator himself pled guilty in exchange for a five-year sentence at the Plymouth County Jail.

Soon after his 1924 release (a year early for good behavior), the onetime millionaire was tried for a slate of state charges and eventually sentenced to a minimum of seven more years. Rather than submitting to the wages of past sins, he faked his suicide and eluded authorities for a short time before being captured aboard a freighter bound for Italy. Upon his second parole in 1934, he was deported as an undesirable alien, leaving behind his beloved Rose and bittersweet memories of his season as the biggest small man in Boston's business scene.

EXECUTION AT
CHARLESTOWN STATE PRISON

- 1927 -

SEARCH BEAMS CREATED THE ILLUSION OF DAYLIGHT in the sky over
Charlestown State Prison, where more than eight hundred police
patrolled the roof, catwalks, yard, and perimeter. Machine guns stood
poised to halt the advance of agitators, and police boats cruised the
same river Paul Revere had rowed across before starting his midnight
ride. To the protestors, liberty was no less under siege the evening of
August 22, 1927, than it had been on April 18, 1775. But this time,
the abusers of justice represented America, and their victims were two
Italian immigrants slated for execution at midnight.

Inside the prison, Nicola Sacco and Bartolomeo Vanzetti awaited
their fate alongside a thief named Celestino Madeiros, who had earlier confessed to the murders for which Sacco and Vanzetti had been
condemned. Across town, Sacco's wife Rosina kept vigil with
Vanzetti's sister, Luigia, who had recently arrived from Italy to beg for
her brother's life. Both women had visited Governor Alvan Tufts

Fuller at 9:00 P.M., Rosina asking him to look on the case "as a family man," and Luigia exhorting him not to let "America become known as the land of cruelty instead of mercy."

As of 11:00 P.M., Fuller remained in his office. In his anteroom sat a young lawyer named Michael Angelo Musmanno, who had been waiting since 10:35 in the hope that the governor would stay the execution. Fuller admitted Musmanno to the office at 11:03 and announced his intention to concur with the attorney general's decision, which he'd just received by letter. As Musmanno expected, the attorney general had recommended that the execution proceed as planned.

Before leaving, he asked the governor once more if he was against the reprieve. When Fuller said that he was, Musmanno asked, "And on that decision you will stand for all time?"

"For all time," the governor affirmed.

At two minutes past midnight, Celestino Madeiros was led into the execution chamber, followed by Nicola Sacco at 12:11 and Bartolomeo Vanzetti at 12:20. When news that Sacco and Vanzetti were dead reached the apartment where Rosina and Luigia sat, their grief-stricken sobs shattered the stillness of the sleeping neighborhood.

Relatives would not be the only ones to mourn the two accused men, whose supporters vented their anger in demonstrations all over the world. Boston would again gird itself for a riot on the Sunday following the executions, when a funeral procession was planned in the predominantly Italian North End. Since Thursday, the men's bodies had lain in state at Langone's Funeral Home, attracting approximately one hundred thousand viewers over the course of three days. Alongside the usual floral tributes lay wreaths with messages expressing the mood of those in attendance: MASSACHUSETTS THE MURDERER was one; REVENGE another.

Sacco and Vanzetti had been imprisoned for more than six years when the date for their execution was set. They were arrested on

May 5, 1920, and charged with armed robbery and two murders. The crime they'd supposedly committed occurred on April 15, when Frederick A. Parmenter and Alessandro Berardelli were held up by two assailants in dark clothes and capes. Berardelli was guarding Parmenter as he walked down Pearl Street in South Braintree, Massachusetts, carrying enough cash to pay fellow workers at the Slater and Morrill Shoe Company. The caped men began firing immediately, leaving five bullets in Berardelli and two in Parmenter before even attempting to steal the payroll boxes. Joined by a third accomplice, they jumped into a waiting getaway car and sped from the scene, waving a shotgun through the back window to deter would-be captors.

Based on little more than a recovered hat and witness testimony implicating Italians, police arrested Sacco and Vanzetti on a streetcar between Bridgewater and Brockton. They'd aroused suspicion by attempting to collect a stored car from a Bridgewater garage—an act that raised alarms because the car was associated with Ferruccio Coacci and Michael Boda, two other Italians the police had been investigating.

The car wasn't the only link between Sacco, Vanzetti, Boda, and Coacci, however. The four men were also bound by their belief in anarchy—an affinity many felt was the actual reason for Sacco and Vanzetti's arrest. The pair had the misfortune to be apprehended at a time when America was in the throes of the Red Scare, when anarchists and radicals were being rounded up in nationwide raids. Dubbed the Palmer Raids after the Attorney General (Michael Palmer) who ordered them, these mass arrests were high on panic and low on constitutional rights.

If their anarchism made them unsavory in the eyes of the law, their Italian heritage may have worsened their chances with a jury. The foreman of the jury they eventually faced was Walter H. Ripley, a man known for using anti-Italian epithets and for claiming that "if he had the power of it, he would keep [Italians] out of the country."

Ripley's prejudices were common among working-class Americans in the 1920s, when the country was adapting to the massive influx of immigrants that arrived between 1880 and 1915. Many of these newcomers lacked the education and English fluency to rise above the field of manual labor, increasing the competition for jobs like mining, bricklaying, shoemaking (like Sacco, who worked at the 3K Shoe Factory), machining, and peddling (like Vanzetti, who sold fish from a cart).

Already threatened by the growing numbers of foreigners in their neighborhoods and labor unions, many Americans were doubly offended by the thought that some of these foreigners opposed the government. As wage-earning anarchists, Sacco and Vanzetti were easily demonized in the court of public opinion—a trend that may well have invaded the actual courtroom.

Though it cannot be said with absolute certainty that Sacco and Vanzetti were innocent, they faced trial with enough evidence to invoke reasonable doubt. Not only did multiple witnesses attest to the men's alibis for the date of the murders, but the defense was able to undermine the integrity of most of the witnesses for the prosecution.

As for physical evidence, the prosecution's case hinged on two guns discovered on the suspects when they were arrested. The state alleged that Sacco's gun had fired one of the bullets recovered from Berardelli's body, while claiming that Vanzetti's gun was stolen from Berardelli during the holdup. These charges were proven false by two ballistics experts produced by the defense, both of whom denied that test bullets fired from Sacco's gun matched the bullet found at the scene. One of the experts also discredited the claim that Vanzetti's gun had belonged to Berardelli, indicating that repairs reportedly made to Berardelli's gun were not consistent with the condition of Vanzetti's weapon.

Equally damning was the defense's disproof of a third piece of physical evidence: a hat discovered near the crime scene that was alleged to belong to Sacco. When the hat was offered to Sacco to try on in court, it was far too small to fit properly over his head. Though the O. J. Simpson trial many years later would popularize the phrase, "If it doesn't fit, you must acquit," no such logic worked in Sacco and Vanzetti's favor. Despite the strength of their case and the sympathy of their supporters, they were judged guilty on July 14, 1921, and sentenced to death on July 10, 1927.

No less than eight appeals were filed and rejected in the intervening six years, as the men's plight assumed the stature of an international cause. During this period, Celestino Madeiros admitted his involvement in the South Braintree robbery, clearing Sacco and Vanzetti of any connection to the crime in a confession he sent to Sacco by messenger. (They were imprisoned in the same jail at the time.) Though Madeiros had everything to lose from this confession, since he was awaiting an appeal for another crime, authorities refused to take it seriously or reconsider Sacco and Vanzetti's case based on its existence. As a former member of the Morelli gang, a professional group of criminals that had been active in South Braintree, Madeiros was a credible suspect for the crime, but the presiding judge declined to evaluate evidence provided by a witness he deemed unreliable.

In response to an avalanche of mail exhorting him to stay the executions, Governor Fuller appointed three prominent men to review the accumulated evidence of the trial, appeals, and denials. These men were Abbott Lowell, president of Harvard University; Samuel Wesley Stratton, president of the Massachusetts Institute of Technology, and former judge Robert Grant. Their review of the case was known as the Lowell Commission. It took these men approximately two months to prepare a twenty-page report, in which they concluded that, "on the whole," Sacco and Vanzetti were "guilty beyond a reasonable doubt" and deserved to be executed.

A different verdict was rendered by the throngs of mourners who followed the hearses toward Forest Hills cemetery, their progress thwarted by the actions of police. Wearing armbands inscribed with the message, JUSTICE CRUCIFIED: AUGUST 22, 1927, the funeral procession strode arm-in-arm through obstacles including club-wielding patrolmen, oncoming traffic, and gangs of hecklers. At the cemetery, Sacco and Vanzetti were cremated while their closest family members remained in the car, ceding the eulogy to Mary Donovan, a member of the Sacco-Vanzetti Defense Committee.

More eloquent than her words was the statement Vanzetti delivered at the sentencing hearing, where he said:

> *I would not wish to a dog or to a snake . . . what I have had to suffer for things that I am not guilty of. But my conviction is that I have suffered for things that I am guilty of. I am suffering because I am a radical and indeed I am a radical; I have suffered because I am an Italian, and indeed I am an Italian; I have suffered more for my family and for my beloved than for myself; but I am so convinced to be right that if you could execute me two times and I could be reborn two other times, I would live again to do what I have done already.*

THE GREAT BRINK'S HEIST

- 1950 -

Brink's, Incorporated employee Charles Grell was nearing the end of his shift when he heard the muffled command, "Okay, boys, put them in the air." The voice issued from one of seven men standing just beyond the barrier separating the vault room from the payroll counting room. The men were armed and costumed to resemble Brink's guards, in navy peacoats and chauffeur's caps. They wore the rubber masks of cartoon gangsters and comic book heroes, but it wasn't Halloween, and this was no prank.

"Come on, get 'em up," one gunman urged Grell, who kneeled before an open vault housing more than $3.5 million. His choices were to reach for the gun in his shoulder holster or to follow the instructions of the lead robber, who ordered him to unlock the gate barring the intruders from the vault.

"Open up, Charlie," one of his fellow guards counseled him, and moments later all five employees were bound, gagged, and stripped of their guns and glasses. So began the "crime of the century," a robbery so masterful that the FBI later pronounced it "perfect."

The site of the heist was a three-story garage building in the North End, where Brink's had moved its vault on December 8, 1948. Before that, its Boston headquarters had been at 80 Federal Street, and it was here that a local burglar named Tony "Fats" Pino first began studying its employees' routines and the routes of its armored cars.

Over the course of four years, Pino came to the conclusion that Brink's—famed for its state-of-the-art security and supposed impenetrability to robbers—was a "sloppy outfit" that was begging to be relieved of its cash. Once the company moved to the North Terminal Garage on 165 Prince Street, he spent another two years casing the new building, leading reconnaissance missions into its offices on an almost nightly basis. In anticipation of an elaborate, multifaceted heist, Pino assembled a group of fellow figures from Boston's underworld, recruiting them for their expertise in safe-cracking, getaway driving, armed robbery, money laundering, and other relevant specialities.

The final crew included Pino, Thomas Francis "Sandy" Richardson, Vincent James Costa (Pino's brother-in-law), John Adolph "Jazz" Maffie, Michael Vincent Geagan, Jimma Faherty, Joseph McGinness, Barney Banfield, Stanley "Gus" Gusciora, Joseph James "Specs" O'Keefe, and Henry Baker. As Pino's knowledge of Brink's evolved, so did his plans for taking its money. At 80 Federal Street, he had targeted the original safe before switching his sights to the armored trucks. The wily grifter had even traced the fleet back to a garage in Cambridge, where he managed to make copies of the keys for every truck in circulation.

For a while, he and his cronies contented themselves with unlocking Brink's trucks and lifting whatever cash they could carry without being noticed. They next upgraded to robbing the safes of the companies served by Brink's, utilizing their knowledge of the trucks and the size of the payrolls they generally delivered. By the time Brink's pulled up its stakes at 80 Federal, Pino had master-minded raids on just about every aspect of its operations except the safe. Upon discovering the company's new North End address, he became more obsessed than ever with the vulnerable vault and its sacks of money, and more firmly convinced that Brink's was beckon-ing him to breach its security system.

Pino's courtship of the score became literal one winter evening in 1949, when he ventured into the inner sanctum of Brink's new offices and "laid a smacker" on the mammoth vault. An accom-plished safecracker with many lesser heists to his name, Pino had always believed that "if you can see a safe face to face, you can crack her." There was just one snag standing between him and his proof of this theory: a small sticker bearing the logo of ADT (American Dis-trict Telegraph), which any experienced robber would recognize as a warning that the vault was wired for alarm.

Despite the gang's best efforts, this obstacle could not be sur-mounted. After an exhaustive campaign to read the safe's combina-tion with implements including naval binoculars and a Bausch and Lomb spotting telescope, Pino dispatched two henchmen (O'Keefe and Gusciora) to the local offices of ADT, where they retrieved a folder containing details on the Brink's alarm system. Next a former MIT student named Sullivan was enlisted to explain the alarm—a task that necessitated a trip to Washington to examine the system's original patent. Even after rifling the patent office for every scrap of information on the so-called Phonetalarm, Sullivan was stumped as to how the device could be disabled.

This impasse was behind Pino's decision to take Brink's "on the heavy," using guns and approaching while the vault was already open. With this aim, he spent countless hours on the roof of a tenement building across the street, deducing the movements of Brink's employees from the order in which the lights shut off. Since most of the cronies he'd recruited were petty criminals who, like him, had no desire to add murder to their résumés, it was important to minimize the possibility of gunplay. For this reason, he concocted a scheme whereby Jimmy Costa would serve as a sentinel, alerting the robbers to the conditions inside the vault room while stationed atop the neighboring tenement building—Pino's home away from home for the bulk of 1949.

By the night of January 17, 1950, the thieves had practiced every aspect of the heist, often staging their rehearsals inside Brink's for authenticity's sake. Pino had removed the cylinders from every essential lock in the building, replacing them with fakes until he had time to mint his own keys at a locksmith around the corner. Using these keys allowed the robbers to invade every sector of the building at will—a strategy they used during multiple attempts leading up to the actual robbery.

While previous runs had failed based on the vault being closed early or employees staying late, the night of the big heist struck Pino as a perfect one for "crooking." A threatened blizzard had failed to materialize, leaving a convenient veil of fog in its stead, and the streets of the North End were unusually empty despite the fact that the Celtics were playing at Boston Garden. (The arena's proximity often caused congestion in the neighborhood.)

As plotted over endless nights on the roof, in the garage, at his Dorchester home and at his criminal "plant" on Blue Hill Avenue, Pino remained on the street waiting in a modified truck with getaway driver Banfield, while Costa cased Brink's from the roof across the street. Meanwhile Maffie, Gusciora, Geagan, Richardson, Faherty, O'Keefe, and Baker crept up the stairs leading to the North Terminal Garage. McGinness, who was responsible mainly for hiding the money once it was stolen, remained at the register of his Dorchester package store.

When Costa saw through his binoculars that the vault was still open and lights in all but the vault room were off, he signaled the seven men below to proceed. At his Copp's Hill elevation, he was blocks away from the famous belfry where two lanterns were hung on April 18, 1775. While those lanterns warned patriots in Charlestown that the British were approaching by water, Costa's flashlight assured a contemporary band of rebels that the coast was clear for "crooking."

It took them less than an hour to empty the vault of some $1,218,211.19 in cash and an additional $1.5 million in checks, money orders, and other securities. Leaving behind only some rope and a signature chauffeur's cap as evidence, they scattered across town like a sack of spilled marbles, some adjourning to the plant to count the cash while others paraded in public to establish their alibis. Pino had the fortune of walking by McGinness's package store while "Big Joe" was chatting with an off-duty policeman, thereby convincing the law that he'd been in Dorchester during the interlude when the heist took place.

Both police and the FBI participated in the investigation that followed—a colossal manhunt that consumed six years and more than twenty-nine million dollars. In the end, the crime was "solved" when "Specs" O'Keefe spilled the beans eleven days before the statute of limitations ran out. Along with Gusciora, O'Keefe had been caught for another series of crimes in Pennsylvania, and his legal fees for these charges had left his family penniless. Convinced that he'd been shortchanged on his take for the Brink's robbery, he blackmailed the other robbers into contributing some fifty thousand dollars to his defense fund. This strategy proved bad for his health, and soon afterward he dodged two murder attempts at the hands of an assassin named Elmer "Trigger" Burke. Whether it was the machine-gun fire, disenchantment with his partners in crime, or the fact that he faced multiple convictions in Pennsylvania and Massachusetts,

O'Keefe divulged the names of every last conspirator in the Brink's heist, and they were all (except for Banfield and Gusciora, who were dead, and "Specs" himself, who earned leniency by confessing) sentenced to life in prison on October 9, 1956.

This brought down the curtain on one of the splashiest chapters in Boston's crime blotter—where it seemed that a handful of wily underdogs had outwitted America's most impregnable security company, escaping with untold riches and the honor of staging the biggest heist ever committed. As affectionate toward its villains as it is toward its heroes, the city was almost saddened by the robbers' downfall. After their arrest, a headline in the *Boston Evening Globe* expressed the awe of its average readers, announcing, WOULD HAVE BEEN FREE: IN 5 DAYS, BRINK'S ROBBERS COULD HAVE TOLD THE WORLD.

DESALVO ESCAPES FROM PRISON

- 1967 -

ARTHUR VINCENT AND HIS SISTER, SIMONE FEDAS, were up late watching a movie when they heard a creaking sound from the direction of the street. Like most other Bostonians with access to newspapers, television, or radio, the siblings were aware that the city's most notorious criminal was at large, having escaped from Bridgewater State Hospital the previous night. What they didn't know—and did not discover until the following afternoon, when he'd surrendered himself to authorities in Lynn—was that this criminal, the internationally reviled Boston Strangler, had just entered their basement and was sifting through their storage bins for a suitable disguise.

After a cursory inspection of the premises, Vincent and Fedas dismissed the noise as a flapping shutter or, at worst, a break-in at the neighborhood liquor store. Meanwhile, their uninvited visitor rummaged through their bins and discovered an old sailor's uniform that was almost his size. Not bad, decided Albert DeSalvo, professed murderer of thirteen women and rapist of hundreds more. Having resolved the pressing issue of what to wear the next day, he settled down on a pile of old newspapers and rags and went to sleep.

DeSalvo's escape catalyzed a manhunt the likes of which Massachusetts hadn't seen since the early 1960s, when the Boston Strangler's killings terrorized the city. With the memory of the murders still fresh in their minds, local women were nearly hysterical at the thought of DeSalvo on the loose, and the media did little to comfort them. While newspapers like the *Boston Record American* warned women to lock their doors and stay inside, rumors circulated that the prisoner had been spotted as far away as Washington, D.C., and Pittsburgh, Pennsylvania. Other, more menacing rumors implied that DeSalvo was en route to a plastic surgeon, to alter his appearance so he could walk the streets undetected.

A red alert went out to every law enforcement agency on the local and national level, and the Boston Police were joined by entities including the Royal Canadian Mounted Police, the FBI, border patrols, and customs officials. This nationwide dragnet did little to console the women of Boston, many of whom installed new locks, purchased attack dogs, checked into hotels (motivated by the fact that the Strangler had never struck at a hotel), or left town altogether. As helicopters circled above and police dogs sniffed their way down alleys and into abandoned buildings, DeSalvo waited in the cellar until midmorning on February 25.

When he left the Vincent-Fedas residence, he had exchanged his telltale prison uniform for the garb of a sailor. He later boasted about the fact that he'd made no effort to reach Ms. Fedas, despite having seen her name printed above the doorbell. It was the kind of courtesy he had shown few women in the past, when he'd professed to sex crimes numbering in the thousands.

Who was DeSalvo, and how had he attained the status of America's most wanted fugitive? According to the State of Massachusetts and his own testimony, he was a psychopathic killer that held Boston under siege between June 14, 1962, and January 4, 1964, murdering single women between the ages of nineteen and eighty-five. The apparent randomness of the Strangler's victims made his rampage all the more terrifying. Considered together, the victims were "Everywoman"—young and old, stocky and slender, black and white, innocent and experienced.

DeSalvo, without doubt, was a sexual predator, having been identified by countless women as both the "Measuring Man" and the "Green Man"—two nicknames for a prolific sex criminal who was active in Massachusetts, Connecticut, New Hampshire, and Rhode Island. As the Measuring Man, he had weaseled his way into the apartments of local coeds, telling them that he was canvassing for models. On the pretext of taking their measurements, he'd grope them thoroughly before leaving with a promise of further contact "from the agency."

His exploits as the Green Man (so named because he always appeared in green work pants) were far more sinister. In this guise, he would break into the apartments of single women and assault them sexually, often apologizing afterward. But when DeSalvo was apprehended for these crimes in November 1964, authorities received a bonus they never expected—and one they never proved, despite exhaustive efforts by policemen, psychiatrists, handwriting experts, forensic investigators, attorneys, statesmen, and even psychics. For the man they had caught was also admitting to a killing spree that had claimed thirteen women. Unprovoked, he was offering a solution to crimes that had panicked the city and confounded the police.

Though DeSalvo confessed in detail to each of the eleven "official" murders and two others, investigators were never able to link him to the crimes through physical evidence. Another prisoner, George Nassar (a man charged with the cold-blooded killing of a gas station attendant), was responsible for bringing the confession to light, and approaching his lawyer (rising star F. Lee Bailey, who later defended DeSalvo) with information that his fellow inmate might be the Strangler. Some who dispute DeSalvo's claims believe that Nassar was the actual Strangler—a criminal so cunning that he persuaded the weaker man to confess, convincing him that his story would earn him a sizable reward and a lucrative book deal.

As film noir as this hypothesis sounds, there is nearly as much evidence to support it as there is for the theory that DeSalvo actually committed the crimes. With his suggestible nature and steel-trap memory, he could easily have been coached in his testimony by Nassar. As Bailey himself reported in *The Defense Never Rests,* DeSalvo's reasons for confessing were simple. He had informed the attorney at their first meeting, "I know I'm going to have to spend the rest of my life locked up somewhere. I just hope it's a hospital, and not a hole like [Bridgewater]. But if I could tell my story to somebody who could write it, maybe I could make some money for my family."

Even to those most involved with the Strangler investigation, this self-effacing sad sack hardly seemed capable of masterminding multiple murders without getting caught. Some investigators doubted that the crimes were the work of one man, believing the older women to have been murdered by one man while the young ones were killed by another. Still others suspected separate culprits for every crime, as news spread of the Strangler's "style" and copycat setups became easier to master.

Confusing the issue further is the fact that DeSalvo was never convicted of the crimes he confessed to. With the intent of shielding him from the possibility of execution, Bailey brought his client to trial for his crimes as the Green Man, attempting to prove him insane by introducing the Strangler murders as evidence. "Certainly the problem was unusual," Bailey later wrote. "I wanted the right to defend a man for robbery and assault by proving that he had committed thirteen murders." In so doing, the attorney believed he could secure a verdict of not guilty by reason of insanity, thereby getting DeSalvo committed to a psychiatric facility where he could be studied.

This strategy backfired on Bailey when the jury found his client guilty on all counts, delivering a sentence of life in prison. DeSalvo felt betrayed by the system and abandoned by those who had coaxed his confession—a situation he sought to "dramatize" with his subsequent breakout. Unfortunately, the plan only dramatized the lax conditions at Bridgewater State Hospital, hastening his transfer to the maximum security Walpole State Prison. Six years after his conviction and subsequent escape, DeSalvo was found dead in the prison's infirmary, having been stabbed repeatedly in the heart by a killer who was never caught.

During his day and a half at large, DeSalvo did not act like the deranged serial killer he claimed to be. In the predawn hours before Boston woke to the news of his escape, he stole a car with the two inmates he'd broken out with (an armed robber named George Harrison and a convicted wife killer named Frederick Erickson) and drove toward Boston. When Harrison and Erickson suggested breaking into a house and holding a family hostage, DeSalvo vetoed the idea, saying, "We're not going to hurt nobody."

After a brief reunion with his brothers Joseph and Richard, he parted ways with the other prisoners and spent the day riding public transportation, tracking the search for the Strangler on a transistor radio he had with him. By the time he sought shelter in the Vincent-Fedas basement, two rewards had been offered for his capture: one for five thousand dollars from the *Boston Record American,* which wanted him dead or alive, and ten thousand dollars from his former attorney, F. Lee Bailey, who specified that his client must be captured alive.

Dressed in his outdated sailor's clothes, DeSalvo surrendered the next day, walking into the Simon Uniform Store and asking for a phone "to call F. Lee." A crowd gathered on the street as he waited with the salesmen for the police to arrive. Some people shouted, "Kill him!" but he was arrested without violence, only to be murdered at Walpole, while in the custody of the State of Massachusetts.

Though DeSalvo never realized his ambition of profiting from his confession, his story proved profitable to countless others who were connected to the case. A postscript was added to his biography in 2001, when the remains of the Strangler's last victim were exhumed for DNA testing at the request of her family. Professor James Starrs and a team of forensic specialists conducted the tests, which indicated that Albert DeSalvo was not responsible for the rape and murder of Mary Sullivan. Whether this means that his confession was a complete fabrication or merely a partial one may never be known, but it suggests that Sullivan's killer was on the loose long before DeSalvo shocked the city with his brief escape.

BOSTON BURNS
OVER FORCED BUSING

- 1974 -

THE SOUND OF HELICOPTERS CUT THROUGH THE CALM of the autumn morning, interrupting the restless sleep of Charlestown's parents and children. More jolting than any alarm clock, the hovering police choppers announced the start of a day residents had resisted with marches, rallies, litigation, and civil disobedience. The failure of these efforts was reflected in the snipers on the roof of Charlestown High School and the hundreds of police on the ground. Some clad in standard uniforms, others in leather jackets and riot gear, they were here to enforce a law many "townies" regarded as the realization of their worst fears. For September 8, 1974, was the first day of school in Boston, and the formal start of a federal plan that required forced busing between urban neighborhoods.

In theory, this plan was designed to improve the racial balance of the city's schools. In practice, it had brought Boston to the brink of a race war, as parents from the impoverished communities of

Charlestown and South Boston raged against the ruling and what it meant for their children. Rather than comply with the law, which ordered reciprocal busing between predominantly black Roxbury and the overwhelmingly white population of Charlestown and "Southie," many white parents refused to send their kids to school at all. So it was that the streets of Charlestown were mobbed by angry parents and truant children when the first buses rolled up Breed's Hill, filled with frightened black students from Roxbury.

Escorted by police, the buses were greeted by jeering, racist posters and hostile shouting. While authorities restrained protestors in the vicinity of the high school, violence and vandalism erupted on Charlestown's less policed streets. An effigy labeled NIGGER BEWARE! was thrown off the roof of the Bunker Hill housing project, then set ablaze in the street below. Elsewhere kids pelted police with rocks, beer bottles, and other rubble, and in the afternoon a crowd of approximately three hundred marched toward Breed's Hill, overturning several cars and setting fire to one of them. One of the worst assaults occurred when irate townies invaded the lobby of Bunker Hill Community College, where they pounced upon a black student and pummeled him, leaving him with an injured arm.

A similar scene was unfolding in South Boston, where the Roxbury buses were waylaid by mobs of screaming, rock-hurling demonstrators. Footage of the riot was broadcast all over the world, depicting the "Cradle of Liberty" as a crucible of racial intolerance. The most damning—and enduring—image of the struggle was shot after the first flush of violence, during a joint march on City Hall by white students from Charlestown and South Boston. When an African-American attorney named Theodore Landsmark crossed the students' path, they beat him to the ground and continued kicking him until he managed to rise to his feet.

What followed was an incident whose ugliness came to define the antibusing crisis: As Landsmark fought to free himself, one student held his arms while another rushed him, aiming the pole of an American flag at his heart.

This attack, as captured in a photograph that won the Pulitzer Prize for spot news photography, stood out in direct contrast to the ideals enshrined on Boston's Black Heritage Trail, where one finds an outpost of the Underground Railroad and a monument honoring the Massachusetts Fifty-fourth (the first black regiment to fight in the Civil War). Having been on the vanguard of the abolitionist movement, Boston was now behind the curve when it came to civil rights—or at least it looked that way from the mass hysteria over desegregation.

Another vivid illustration of this shift came when Senator Ted Kennedy, a defender of court-ordered desegregation, made an impromptu appearance at an antibusing rally, where he was shouted down and pelted with food by constituents who had once supported him. Amid generalized insults and calls for his impeachment, one heckler shouted, "Why don't you let them shoot you, like they shot your brother!" This callous reference to John F. Kennedy showed that no icon was too sacred to be toppled in the antibusing frenzy. Regarding busing as a scheme supported by sanctimonious liberals, the crowd harbored no sympathies for Senator Kennedy, who sent his own kids to private school while theirs were being bused to Roxbury.

It was this inequity that was at the heart of the antibusing furor, which was less about racism than it was about class. The communities targeted by the federal busing order were among the city's most disadvantaged and educationally deprived. Schools in white working-class Charlestown and South Boston were no better than schools in black working-class Roxbury, yet the order decreed that a certain percentage of students in each neighborhood must leave their local schools for hostile, equally unpromising academic environments. To the struggling parents, the ruling seemed an unjust trespass on their right to control their own children.

The groundwork for forced busing was laid in 1965, when the Advisory Committee on Racial Imbalance and Education recommended legislation to improve the integration of Boston's schools. "Separation from others breeds ignorance of others," the statement read, proposing that this separation be addressed through measures including "the exchange of students between other school buildings."

After years of charges and countercharges between Boston's School Committee and supporters of the Racial Imbalance Act, the decision made its way to the desk of federal judge W. Arthur Garrity Jr. After weighing options both moderate and extreme, Garrity made a ruling designed to impose racial balance on Boston's schools. This would be achieved by the crosstown busing of some twenty-five thousand students—among them the children of South Boston, a white neighborhood known for its hostility to outsiders, and Roxbury, a community widely seen as the center of the city's black ghetto.

The judge could have scarcely found two more economically challenged, culturally incompatible communities on which to impose forced busing. In a preliminary hearing on the proposal, Professor Louis Jaffe urged its architects to reconsider, noting that the pairing of two such communities was destined to provoke violence. Less impartial pleas were voiced by panicked mothers, one of whom voiced her concerns in a meeting of the Governor's Commission on the Status of Women. Citing forced busing as a women's issue, she asked the commission to represent the rights of Boston's mothers. "We are poor women locked into an economically miserable situation," she read from a prepared statement. "All we want is to be mothers to the children God gave us. We are not opposed to the color of anyone's skin. We are opposed to the forced busing of our children to schools other than in our neighborhood."

Uniting in organizations like ROAR (Restore Our Alienated Rights), Massachusetts Citizens Against Forced Busing, and Powder Keg, parents from Southie and Charlestown lobbied Judge Garrity for a reprieve from forced busing. When no such reprieve was granted, demonstrators converged on the judge's home in Wellesley, a wealthy white suburb whose sheltered residents, they argued, had no business deciding the fate of poor children from the inner city.

The legitimacy of their argument was buried in a barrage of racist brutality, but the antibusing crisis was more complicated than the black and white (or white against black) conflict portrayed in the national media. In imposing forced busing on its poorest citizens, the federal ruling did a disservice to the very students it was trying to empower, placing kids of both races at risk.

An ironic postscript to the issue of forced busing came in 1999, when a group of parents sued the U.S. District Court on behalf of four white students, asking that it abandon race-based admission policies in Boston schools. Filed twenty-five years to the day after Judge Garrity's ruling on desegregation, the lawsuit charged that the current system discriminates against white children. The School Committee subsequently voted to eliminate race as a consideration in school assignments, signaling a return to the "neighborhood schools" championed by Garrity's detractors.

THE GARDNER ART HEIST

- 1990 -

THE STREETS WERE STILL RAUCOUS WITH Saint Patrick's Day revelers when the twenty-three-year-old musician checked in for his midnight shift at the Isabella Stewart Gardner Museum. Being a night watchman was "the most boring job in the world" to the Berklee College of Music student, but it paid reasonably well and allowed him to spend his days practicing and his evenings playing in rock clubs. Tonight his usual partner in misery, a much older veteran guard, had called in sick and been replaced by a twenty-five-year-old horn player. So it was that two novices were on the job when the intercom buzzed at 1:24 A.M., rung by two mustachioed gentlemen dressed in the uniforms of the Boston Police.

Citing a "disturbance on the grounds," the unexpected visitors demanded access to the museum's interior courtyard—an oasis of statuary and exotic plants at the center of the fifteenth-century Venetian-style palace. Since the horn player was doing his rounds on the third floor, it was up to the younger guard to decide whether to buzz the "officers" through the locked security doors. Convinced of their authority, he let them in—and by 1:48 he and his colleague were bound in duct tape and tied to posts in the museum's basement, helpless to intervene as two thieves roamed the treasure-packed floors above.

It took less than an hour for the men to complete the biggest art theft in American history, stripping the museum of thirteen pieces valued at roughly three hundred million dollars. Their path was traced by the Gardner's motion detector system—an ineffective security device since the museum didn't have enough guards, alarms, and other adequate security measures. They focused their efforts on the second floor, where one man stripped a Vermeer and three of four Rembrandts from the Dutch Room, while the other plundered five Degas sketches from the Short Gallery. Among the other priceless works collected in their rampage were Govaert Flinck's *Landscape with an Obelisk* (an oil painting then believed to be a Rembrandt), Manet's *Chez Tortoni* (the sole painting taken from the first floor's Blue Room), a Chinese beaker made of bronze, and a finial featuring a gilded eagle, which they apparently swiped as a consolation prize after failing to remove the Napoleonic banner that came with it.

Part of the heist's fascination stems from the provenance of the artworks—and the peculiar intimacy of the space from which they were stolen. Unlike the Museum of Fine Arts nearby, the Gardner is in every sense a personal collection, bearing the stamp of its founder, Isabella Stewart Gardner. To visit the Gardner is to imagine oneself as a guest of the charismatic "Mrs. Jack" (so-called in connection to her husband, financier John L. "Jack" Gardner). In the days when she presided over the imposing structure known as Fenway Court, her visitors included luminaries like James McNeill Whistler, Henry James, and John Singer Sargent, whose portraits of her can be seen in the first-floor Macknight Room *(Mrs. Gardner in White)* and the third-floor Gothic Room *(Portrait of Isabella Stewart Gardner).*

One of her era's most prominent arts patrons, Isabella forged her collection over the course of three decades of international travel. To house it, she commissioned the construction of Fenway Court, a four-story showplace modeled on residences she'd admired in Venice. With its grand fireplaces and ornate furniture, the museum seems less like a repository for fine art than an exquisite home whose owner has stepped out for a spell. Adding to its mystique is the fact that she frequently entertained there, staging soirees for leading names of the Gilded Age. If the museum's walls could talk, they would reveal not only the identities of the art thieves but incidental conversations between the likes of actress Sarah Bernhardt, philosopher George Santayana, and Julia Ward Howe, writer of "The Battle Hymn of the Republic."

Upon her death in 1924, Mrs. Gardner left instructions that the exhibits remain on view exactly as she had arranged them. With the notable exception of the theft, these instructions have been heeded ever since its doors opened to the public on the evening of January 1, 1903. On that magical night, when guests were welcomed with a classical concert by members of the Boston Symphony Orchestra, William James compared the experience to "a Gospel miracle," inspired to hyperbole by the "aesthetic perfection" of the galleries and flower-filled courtyard. Despite the upheavals of a war-torn century, much that those first visitors saw remains intact. All but the spaces where the stolen masterpieces once stood, where empty frames and barren pedestals bear witness to the gaps in the collection.

How did it happen? How did two crooks penetrate the inner sanctum of one of the world's most storied museums, absconding with works like *The Concert,* one of only thirty-five existing paintings by Vermeer, and *The Storm on the Sea of Galilee,* Rembrandt's only known seascape? A more appropriate question, in view of the museum's vulnerability on the night of the crime, might be, "Why didn't it happen earlier?" For while administrators adhered slavishly to Gardner's instructions on the placement and preservation of her art, they seem to have had a sizable blind spot where security was concerned.

Improbable as it seems in light of the value of its holdings, the museum had little more protection that night than the average private residence. Granted, there were the motion detectors and four video monitors that apprised guards of activity in and around the grounds. There were the guards themselves, one of whom was a substitute and one of whom, when threatened by the thieves, responded, "Don't worry. They don't pay me enough to get hurt." And there was a single alarm button behind the control desk—an element that was easily bypassed when the "police" ordered the seated guard to show some identification. Even more improbable is the fact that the Gardner carried no insurance policy at the time of the heist—an oversight that has left it unremunerated for the stolen masterpieces. Combined with the fact that the statute of limitations for the theft has expired (making the culprits immune from prosecution), it would seem that the two false policemen got away with the perfect crime.

Because the scene of this crime remains the same as they found it, it is easy to follow their footsteps through the hushed galleries of today's Gardner. In the Dutch Room, they encountered their only obstacle when an alarm sounded as they struggled with a Rembrandt painting in a heavy frame. The baseboard alarm was easily dismantled—they simply smashed it. Upon silencing it, they realized it was only a warning beeper, designed to alert guards when visitors trespassed too close to the artwork.

Despite the knowledge that they had the run of the Gardner's rooms until morning, the thieves wasted little time in completing their conquest. They proceeded methodically, as if working from a list, ripping paintings and drawings from their wall placements and shattering the glass of their frames. Their disrespect for the art they stole has led some to surmise that they were hired hands or gangsters rather than motivated art thieves, for what art lover could cut *The Storm on the Sea of Galilee* from its frame and knock *The Concert* and *Chez Tortoni* from their settings? Even more telling is the fact that they completely skipped the third floor, where the museum's most valuable collection was (and remains) on view in the Titian Room. Their avoidance of the celebrated painting, Titian's *The Rape of Europa,* points either to an assignment involving specific works (commissioned, perhaps, by an amoral collector obsessed with Rembrandt and Degas) or total ignorance of the museum's holdings and their value on the black market.

Whatever their motives, the thieves terminated their mission at 2:28 A.M., checking on the guards in the basement before extracting the tapes from the video monitors and seizing the computer printout from the motion detector system (which had nevertheless captured their movements on its hard drive). It took them two trips to load some of the century's most priceless art into their getaway vehicle, and in their wake they left shattered glass, scraps of canvas, and the splintered remains of wood casings. It was the most audacious art theft ever committed, and its perpetrators had accomplished it without weapons.

Since then investigators have continued to seek solutions to the Gardner art heist. Rumors have implicated an accomplished art thief (Myles Connor, who was jailed at the time but is suspected of conceiving and planning the crime), an infamous gangster (James "Whitey" Bulger, whose career in organized crime was at its peak in 1990), and the Irish Republican Army (which has a track record for international art theft). All of these leads have proven to be red herrings, as have tips suggesting that the stolen works have been spotted in Japan and the Charlestown Navy Yard (in both instances, the paintings in question were reproductions).

Every few years, the case resurfaces in the news, often after investigators or museum staffers have been contacted by someone claiming to have access to the stolen art. Since none of these claims have yielded results, visitors to the museum can only speculate on the location of the missing masterpieces. Though the museum suffered a staggering monetary and aesthetic loss on the morning of March 18, 1990, the art-loving public is most affected by the theft of these works, which were ripped from the settings selected by Mrs. Gardner and removed to a place (or places) where they can only be viewed illicitly, if at all.

WHITEY BULGER'S DISAPPEARING ACT

- 1995 -

As endings go, it was more of a whimper than a bang: a final act from which the lead actor was missing. After multiple attempts by both state and federal law enforcement agencies, prosecutors were finally prepared to press charges against the elusive boss of Boston's Irish mob, taking him down in a dragnet that included his longtime lieutenant, Steve "The Rifleman" Flemmi, and an associate named "Cadillac" Frank Salemme. But though the Rifleman was apprehended with relative ease outside a Quincy Market restaurant and Cadillac Frank turned up eight months later in West Palm Beach, Florida, the indictment's prime target was nowhere to be found. Leaving behind a rap sheet with charges ranging from money laundering to eighteen counts of murder, the gangster known as James "Whitey" Bulger had slipped through the fingers of the law yet again.

This kind of narrow escape was something of a habit for Bulger, who'd spent more than thirty years honing his reputation as the Houdini of Boston's crime scene. Investigations had been mounted against him by the Massachusetts State Police, the Boston Police Department, the Quincy Police Department, the Drug Enforcement Agency, and independent detectives as far away as Tulsa, Oklahoma, but all of these cases had come to nothing, leaving Bulger unscathed while countless others went to prison. The once formidable local branch of LCN (La Cosa Nostra, or Italian mafia) had all but imploded during Bulger's lengthy criminal career, but the South Boston–bred gangster had barely had a parking ticket since his release from prison in 1965.

The reason for his invincibility was revealed in the subsequent court case against Flemmi and Salemme. In a hearing on May 22, 1997, a Justice Department official named Paul Coffey was called to the stand. Under oath, Coffey dropped a bombshell on the unsuspecting audience, revealing that "James J. Bulger was an informant for the Boston division of the Federal Bureau of Investigation," and had been for some twenty years. Suddenly the mob boss's immunity to arrest made sense: Though painted as the ultimate wiseguy, Bulger's survival had nothing to do with wiliness or street smarts. The reason he had prevailed while most of his rivals had not was because Bulger had the backing of the FBI. In exchange for a steady supply of underworld gossip—mostly about people who happened to be in his way—the FBI made sure Bulger stayed on the street, no matter how many crimes he was accused of committing.

It all started in the fall of 1975, when an ambitious FBI agent named John Connolly tapped Bulger about the possibility of becoming a government source. Connolly had grown up in the same South Boston housing project as Whitey and been friends with his older brother William, a powerful politician and the longtime president of the Massachusetts state senate.

The two met in a parked car at Quincy's Wollaston Beach and discussed the landscape of Boston's underworld, which was dominated by the fearsome Gennaro J. Angiulo and his cronies in La Cosa Nostra. As quickly as he had climbed through the ranks of Somerville's Winter Hill gang, Bulger was still second in command to Howie Winter, and Winter in turn was no match for the well-connected Angiulo. Implicit in Connolly's pitch was a means for Bulger to bypass these men in his journey to the top. Why toil in the trenches when a few well-placed words could send Angiulo and company to prison, leaving the path clear for Winter Hill and its heir apparent, Whitey Bulger?

Though it's unclear whether Bulger was aware of it at the time, he wasn't the first Winter Hill gangster to become an informant. Already on the government rolls was Steve "The Rifleman" Flemmi, who had been recruited by agent H. Paul Rico in the mid-1960s. As with Bulger, Flemmi's conversion from stand-up guy to stool pigeon would have been inconceivable to the racketeers, extortionists, killers, and other criminals whose secrets he was reporting to officials. Like Bulger, Flemmi had made his name in Boston by establishing himself as a fearless and reliable henchman. Whether he was encouraging an associate—with the help of a visible weapon—to pay an overdue loan or dumping the body of a less cooperative associate from a moving car, Flemmi had a taste for dirty work and a gift for doing it discreetly.

But if none could have guessed Flemmi's hidden life as "Jack from South Boston" (his FBI code name), the mere mention of Bulger as an informant would have been heresy on the streets of the neighborhood he grew up in. For South Boston was the home of the "Code of Silence," the kind of place where a murder could take place in a crowded bar and nevertheless have no witnesses. Each Bulger brother represented a different aspect of Southie's insular identity, with Senator William lending a public face to the private grievances of hometown constituents while gangster Whitey forged a persona as "a good bad guy"—a criminal so charismatic that many perceived him as a champion rather than a menace.

To the rank-and-file criminals cowering in the wake of this larger-than-life gangster, it was easier to imagine him outsmarting government officials rather than collaborating with them. And in this lay the beauty of Bulger's twenty-year stint as an informant: Of all the criminals at large in Boston at the time, he was the one no one would ever dare suspect of betrayal.

In theory, Bulger and Flemmi's relationship with the FBI was "you scratch my back, I'll scratch yours." In practice, it evolved into more of an "I scratch my back, you scratch my back" equation, as Connolly and company insulated the informants from danger while arresting all of their enemies. In addition to briefing the gangsters on active investigations against them and burying evidence of their crimes in government files, Connolly and his longtime supervisor, John Morris, often socialized with the informants, joining them for lavish meals and eventually accepting cash and other gifts in the guise of friendship. Proof of who was pulling the puppet strings can be seen in the pair's unblemished record during their years as informants—during which they routinely engaged in extortion, racketeering, money laundering, narcotics distribution, torture, and execution-style murder.

Having alerted his "top echelon informant" to everything from efforts to bug his car to underworld rivals who were informing against him, is it any surprise that Connolly came through for Bulger when his luck ran out in 1995? Though the agent had retired at the top of his profession in 1990, credited by some for bringing about La Cosa Nostra's downfall in Boston, Connolly still had enough connections to know that a case was being built against Bulger and Flemmi. As he'd done so many times during their glory days together, he assumed the role of informer to his prize informant, counseling him to stay away from Boston when arrests were being made.

From his position as head of corporate security at Boston Edison, there was little Connolly could do to protect his "good bad" friends from prosecution. When it became clear that this particular investigation could not be deflected, Connolly made sure that Bulger was "on vacation" at the pivotal moment. The vacation became permanent once Flemmi was caught, and Bulger remains on the lam as of this writing, accompanied by his girlfriend, Catherine Greig.

Occasionally one hears of Bulger sightings in places as divergent as New York, Wyoming, Mississippi, and an island off the coast of Louisiana, where he reportedly rented property in 1995 and 1996. In his absence, his legend has only grown larger in Boston, yielding several books and countless screenplays about the gangland kingpin who managed to beat the law by joining it. Ironically, in his transition from ally to outlaw, Bulger has retained his "top echelon" status with the FBI—a status that's reflected in the fact that his mug shot resides next to Osama Bin Laden's on the agency's list of "Top Ten Most Wanted Fugitives."

HERE COME THE BRIDES

- 2004 -

THE BRIDE WORE A WHITE PANTSUIT and a glowing smile as she waited for the moment she'd thought would never come. At forty-six, she had never been married, though she'd been in a committed relationship for seventeen years and mothered a child with her partner. But as long as she had waited to speak them, the vows she'd exchange on May 17, 2004, were merely a formality for Julie Goodridge, who'd seen Hillary Goodridge as her spouse since long before the courts deemed they could be married.

Eight-year-old Annie Goodridge stole the show at the ceremony, wearing an ear-to-ear smile as she performed her dual role as flower girl and ring bearer. Her birth had been the driving factor behind her mothers' decision to sue the Massachusetts Supreme Judicial Court, joining with six other couples in a three-year struggle for the right to be legally wed. For despite their long commitment and shared surname (the maiden name of Hillary's grandmother, which they'd adopted in anticipation of having Annie), Hillary was barred from

Julie's bedside during critical moments of their daughter's birth by cesarean section. In the eyes of the law, Hillary and Julie were not partners, no matter how many years they'd been together and how much history they held in common. Struck by the inequity of their situation and concerned for the stability of Annie's future, the Goodridges set out to change the state's position on same-sex marriage.

The landmark case was handled by Mary Bonauto of Gay and Lesbian Advocates and Defenders, a New England organization dedicated to securing legal rights for those whose sexual orientation, HIV status, and/or gender identity may place them in the path of discrimination. Bonauto, herself a lesbian mother in a longtime relationship, became the country's most prominent advocate for marriage equality, earning comparisons to Supreme Court Justice Thurgood Marshall in the *New York Times*. Likening Bonauto's defense of *Goodridge v. Department of Public Health* to Marshall's defense of *Brown v. Board of Education,* the newspaper equated the fight for same-sex marriage to the fight for desegregation in southern public schools.

Over the course of her career as an attorney, Bonauto had often been asked to assist gay and lesbian couples through legal difficulties they would never have encountered as heterosexual spouses. While husbands and wives took for granted certain rights regarding adoption and child custody, inheritance and Social Security survivor benefits, health benefits coverage and tax relief, these rights were forbidden to gay couples under Massachusetts state law.

One such couple was Hillary and Julie Goodridge, who felt keenly the benefits denied them because of their sexual orientation. "We've done all the legal work we can to protect our rights and the rights of our daughter, but we still can't transfer assets to our spouse, benefit from each other's Social Security should one of us die, and we worry about emergencies when we travel, even with all the proper documentation," Julie noted. "We have a beautiful child, a nice home, and we volunteer at school, but we're still left out. It just doesn't make any sense to us."

With the plight of the Goodridges and countless other committed gay couples "seared into [her] soul," Bonauto filed a suit claiming that Massachusetts had violated its own constitutional equality provisions by refusing to grant marriage licenses to partners of the same sex. When the trial court rejected this claim, she took it to the next level, appealing to the seven justices of the Massachusetts Supreme Judicial Court.

Central to her strategy was a choice not to stand for half-measures, and to demand nothing less than the legalization of marriage for gay couples. Though she (along with two colleagues) had previously secured a decision favoring "civil unions" from the Vermont legislature, Bonauto knew that danger lay in settling for a "separate but equal" judgment. Noting the fact that "civil unions" confer the legal benefits of matrimony without honoring such unions with the name "marriage," she argued, "When it comes to marriage, there really is no such thing as separating the word . . . from the protections it provides. The reason for that is that one of the most important protections of marriage is the word, because the word is what conveys the status that everyone understands as the ultimate expression of love and commitment."

Five months after she made this appeal, the Massachusetts Supreme Judicial Court shocked the world with its decision, a 4–3 ruling that "failed to identify any constitutionally adequate reason" that same-sex couples should not marry. The celebration was equaled only by the backlash, as conservative groups marshaled support for a constitutional amendment that would ban gay marriages in favor of the less symbolically charged option of civil unions. President George W. Bush expressed his displeasure in a subsequent statement, calling marriage "a sacred institution between a man and a woman" and decrying the attempt of "activist judges" to "[redefine] marriage by court order."

These views are echoed by many opponents of same-sex marriage, who favor civil unions only as a last resort to prevent gays and lesbians from marrying. Bolstered by the Bible and other sources extraneous to the Constitution, detractors feel that to legalize same-sex marriage is to endanger the sanctity of marriage itself. For members of organizations like the Massachusetts Family Institute, the allowance of marital benefits to homosexuals sanctions a lifestyle they regard as immoral and an impediment to family values.

While discomfort with homosexuality (and its potential impact on the traditional family) is a strong motivator for opponents of gay marriage, it is not the only one. Mitt Romney, then governor of Massachusetts, expressed the grievances of many when he said that a minority (the state's Supreme Judicial Court) should not impose its will on the majority (Massachusetts voters) when it came to an issue so personal and emotionally charged. "The people of Massachusetts should not be excluded from a decision as fundamental to our society as the definition of marriage," he said in a written statement. "This issue is too important to leave to a one-vote majority of the [court]."

Whatever their objections, opponents of gay marriage would not be able to stop it from happening in Massachusetts. Refusing to consider politicians' proposals that civil unions be approved in lieu of marriage, the court issued an advisory opinion stating, "Because the proposed law by its express terms forbids same-sex couples legal entry into civil marriage, it continues to relegate same-sex couples to a different status . . . The history of our nation has demonstrated that separate is seldom, if ever, equal."

Following the ruling, couples like Hillary and Julie were free to begin planning their weddings. The first marriage licenses were issued to same-sex partners on May 17, 2004, a day designated "marriage destruction day" by angry protestors on City Hall Plaza. Undeterred by the sign-waving, slogan-shouting hecklers, Julie and Hillary swept into City Hall, borne on a tide of news media, police guards, and other gay couples seeking marriage licenses. They were greeted personally by Boston Mayor Thomas Menino, who later staged a wedding reception under a white tent on City Hall Plaza. The festivities easily eclipsed the rally staged by opponents of gay marriage—a testament to communal pride in the fact that, in Menino's words, "Once again, we've broken down a barrier in the city of Boston and the state of Massachusetts."

Clad in matching white pantsuits, Hillary and Julie were finally wed in a 2:00 P.M. ceremony at the Beacon Street headquarters of the Unitarian Universalist Association (UUA). After being pronounced wife and wife by the UUA's president, Reverend William G. Sinkford, they emerged from the church to a shower of rainbow confetti. To the tune of the traditional "Wedding March," friends sang, "Here come the brides, so gay with pride. Long may you be, legally free. Finally hitched by a 4–3 decree."

Though the Goodridges later announced their amicable separation in 2006 (proving themselves equal, even in imperfection, to the heterosexual spouses whose status they sought to share), on their wedding day they happily embodied the hopes of same-sex partners everywhere. Addressing the prospect of a future constitutional amendment that would invalidate the court's decision, Hillary declined political rhetoric, speaking instead from personal experience. "Come on over to our house for dinner," she said to those who perceived gay marriage as a threat to traditional unions. "Find out how loving and normal and boring we are."

THE RED SOX REVERSE THE CURSE

- 2004 -

WITH TWO OUTS, A MAN ON SECOND, and the score at 3–1, Cardinals batter Edgar Renteria swung and connected. The ball hopped once before landing in the mitt of pitcher Keith Foulke, who leapt to catch it as it sailed over his head. The ball securely in his glove, Foulke jogged a few steps toward first base as if he intended to hand deliver it. Such caution would have seemed laughable on any other out, for any other team, in any other game but the fourth in a 3–0 World Series. But Foulke was the closing pitcher for the Red Sox in the ninth inning of a game that would change history, and when he finally tossed the ball to first baseman Doug Mientkiewicz, he slammed the door not only on the Cardinals but on a curse that had plagued Boston for the past eighty-six years.

Eighty-six years since the Red Sox had won a World Series championship. Eighty-four years since they'd sold Babe Ruth to the Yankees, catalyzing a run of bad luck that came to be known as the Curse of the Bambino. In 2004, these numbers became footnotes, mere subtext to a storybook season that had defied all odds, transforming a group of rumpled, badly coiffed misfits into America's team.

In some ways, it was the same team that had confirmed the Curse during the previous season, losing in spectacular fashion to the New York Yankees in Game 7 of the American League Championship Series. After a hard-fought series against a team widely seen as Boston's nemesis, everything seemed to be going Boston's way until the eighth inning of a 5–2 contest. Despite the fact that ace pitcher Pedro Martinez (who was known to flag after 105 pitches) was past his statistical breaking point and had given up three hits and a run in the seventh inning, general manager Grady Little left him in rather than calling a reliever from the bullpen.

What followed would be etched in the memories of long-suffering Red Sox fans, alongside blunders like Johnny Pesky's held ball in 1946 (when his tardy throw allowed the St. Louis Cardinals to score the winning run in the World Series) and Bill Buckner's infamous 1986 fielding error (when he let a ground ball roll between his legs in yet another failed championship quest, this time against the New York Mets). By the end of the inning, the game would be tied, as the exhausted Martinez ceded hit after hit to the stars of the Yankees batting order.

After this reversal of fortune—the latest in nearly nine decades of avoidable errors and unforeseen upsets that had barred Boston from the winner's circle—it came as no surprise when Aaron Boone homered to win the game for the Yankees. Once again, the light at the end of the tunnel for Red Sox fans had turned into an oncoming train. Once again, New York had the last laugh in the storied rivalry, taunting the beaten Sox with cries of "1918" (the last year Boston won the World Series) and banners bearing the smirking likeness of Babe Ruth.

The rivalry only grew hotter in the off-season, as both teams vied for star players in a high-profile bidding war. Addressing flaws in their pitching staff, the Red Sox secured the services of ace Curt Schilling (formerly of the Arizona Diamondbacks) and closer Keith Foulke (who they bought from the Oakland Athletics). In the most heavily hyped transaction of the year, Boston traded Manny Ramirez to the Texas Rangers for All-Star shortstop Alex "A-Rod" Rodriguez, only to have the deal voided by the Major League Baseball Players Association because it entailed a voluntary pay cut for Rodriguez. Where did A-Rod eventually land? In New York, of course, where the Yankees added him to an off-season shopping cart that included starting pitcher Javier Vazquez, All-Star relief pitchers Paul Quantrill and Tom Gordon, speedy center fielder Kenny Lofton, and heavy hitter Gary Sheffield.

Needless to say, the rivalry didn't abate when the season started, and the feud became literal on July 24, when Boston pitcher Bronson Arroyo hit A-Rod on the elbow during a game at Fenway Park. What started as a heated exchange of words between the Yankee batter (who thought the hit was intentional) and Sox catcher Jason Varitek (who maintained Arroyo's innocence) evolved into a bench-clearing brawl when Varitek palmed A-Rod's face with his mitt, lifting him off the ground by one leg as players from both teams rushed the field.

By the time the two teams reprised their roles in the 2004 American League Championship Series, the rivalry had assumed the dimensions of an opera, complete with Pedro Martinez as the temperamental diva and Curt Schilling as the battle-scarred veteran. Other characters seemed imported from a soap opera, like the long-haired, unshaven Johnny Damon (a heartthrob some described as the spitting image of Jesus) and Yankees owner George Steinbrenner, whose big-spending, cutthroat management style would seem right at home on a rerun of *Dynasty*.

Billed as a rematch between bitter enemies, the 2004 ALCS was the culmination of a season's worth of subplots—among them the battered ego of Martinez, who, after winning only six of his last twenty-three starts against them, memorably called the Yankees "my daddy" and admitted, "I can't find a way to beat them at this point." There was the charismatic Damon, who'd described his team as "idiots" in an interview that set the tone for the postseason. There was the venerable Schilling, whose ability to pitch had been jeopardized by a torn tendon sheath in his ankle. And, as always, there was the Bambino, whose spirit hovered over the start of the series at Yankee Stadium.

Game 1 confirmed the worst fears of fans who believed in the Curse. With a hobbled Schilling on the mound, the Red Sox looked outmatched in a 10–7 loss. By Game 3, even the most optimistic fans felt haunted, as first Martinez, then Arroyo led losing campaigns against the Yankees. Babe Ruth's ghost must have been smiling when the final out was made in the third loss, sealing the score at 19–8— a single digit shy of 1918.

In the media, the series may as well have been over, as Boston reporters lamented the sheer hopelessness of the situation. On the eve of Game 4, the *Boston Globe*'s Dan Shaughnessy wrote, "So there. For the eighty-sixth consecutive autumn, the Red Sox are not going to win the World Series. No baseball team in history has recovered from a 3–0 deficit, and this most promising Sox season in eighteen years could be officially over tonight. Mercy."

Shaughnessy and others would have to eat their words when the Red Sox engineered one of the most remarkable comebacks in sports history, pulling even with the Yankees behind the pitching of Schilling, Martinez, and the suddenly unstoppable Derek Lowe. In an episode of particular interest to "Curse mongers," an orthopedic specialist named Bill Morgan performed an unprecedented surgical procedure on Schilling so he could pitch in Game 6. Before operating on the pitcher in the Red Sox clubhouse, however, Dr. Morgan practiced the procedure on a human cadaver, leading some to say that the dead were raised to pave the way for a Red Sox victory.

Schilling pitched with a bloody sock, as the stitches securing his tendon began to pop out. It was an image among many that came to define this unforgettable series: instant icon David "Big Papi" Ortiz pointing to the heavens after one of his game-breaking home runs, A-Rod slapping the ball out of Arroyo's mitt in a desperate ploy to avoid an out, and finally the Red Sox celebrating their American League championship in Yankee Stadium, also known as the "House That Ruth Built."

After this cinematic series, with its emotional highs and lows, the World Series itself seemed anticlimactic. The Red Sox had beaten their archenemies in the most dramatic fashion possible, emerging from a 0–3 hole to win after obituaries had been posted in the national media. The St. Louis Cardinals were an estimable team, and they owned the winningest record in baseball in 2004. But as rivals, they lacked the baggage, the menace, and the mettle of the Yankees, and the Red Sox swept them in four straight games.

The game that officially reversed the Curse was played under a lunar eclipse, on the eighty-sixth anniversary of their World Series victory in 1918. When first baseman Mientkiewicz tagged Renteria for the final out, catcher Jason Varitek leapt into the arms of Foulke, the closer. Soon the dugout emptied onto the field as Joe Castiglione, the Red Sox radio announcer, shouted, "The Red Sox are World Champions. Can you believe it?"

It was a moment that countless Red Sox fans had lived their whole lives in hope of seeing, and all over New England parents woke their children so they could witness history. Over the past eighty-six years, fans had grown accustomed to having their hearts broken, and extremists had attempted to break the spell by staging exorcisms, diving for Babe Ruth's piano (which had been tossed in a pond by the Bambino in 1918), and placing a Red Sox cap at the summit of Mount Everest. But all the bad luck and blighted dreams disappeared on October 27, 2004, leaving Boston to adjust to its new identity: that of a championship contender, whose chances were suddenly no worse—or better—than those of any other team.

BOSTON FACTS & TRIVIA

Boston derives its name from an English city originally called Botolphston, which in turn was named for a seventh-century abbot, Saint Botolph. Located in Lincolnshire, Botolphston (later shortened to Boston) was home to many of Massachusetts's first Puritan settlers.

A statue of Leif Ericson stands on the Commonwealth Avenue mall, commemorating the unsubstantiated rumor that the Norse explorer visited the Bay State on an early visit to America (ca. 1000). The rumor stems from Ericson's description of a landscape similar to Boston's encompassing a river (the Charles) running through a lake (the Back Bay) into the sea (Boston Harbor).

The first known inhabitants of Boston were eastern Algonquin Indians, among them the Massachusetts, Nipmucks, Pocumtucks, and Wampanoags (or Pokanokets). Around 1615–1619, 80 to 90 percent of New England's Native Americans were killed by a series of epidemics stemming from diseases imported by Europeans.

As a city of firsts, Boston is unrivaled, having originated America's first public park (Boston Common, 1634), public school (Boston Latin, 1635), college (Harvard, 1636), post office (1639), lighthouse (Boston Light, 1716), chocolate factory (Walter Baker Company, 1765), swimming pool (1827), public library (1854), subway (1897), and marathon (April 19, 1897), among others.

Some may find it surprising that Boston was also the site of the first divorce in America, granted to Ann Clark (whose husband had fathered two children with her—and two with another woman) in 1643.

Though he is most closely associated with Baltimore, the author Edgar Allan Poe was born in Boston in 1809. He later observed of the city, after returning for an unfavorably reviewed reading of "The Raven," "We like Boston. We were born there . . . and perhaps it is just as well not to mention that we are heartily ashamed of the fact."

The "real" Uncle Sam hailed from a Boston suburb, according to the 1961 United States Congress, which assigned the title to Arlington's Samuel Wilson for supplying U.S.-stamped beef to American troops during the War of 1812.

The oldest commissioned ship in the U.S. Navy resides in the Charlestown Navy Yard, berth of the U.S.S. *Constitution*. Also known as "Old Ironsides," the undefeated warship earned her nickname during a skirmish in the War of 1812, when she withstood a barrage from the British frigate *Guerriere*. As cannonball after cannonball bounced off the oak vessel, one of her crew was heard to exclaim, "Huzza, her sides are made of iron!"

In 1872, the Great Boston Fire raged for four days, destroying 776 buildings on sixty-five acres in the center of town. Fourteen died in the conflagration, which started in the basement of a dry goods store on Summer Street.

Another little-known first occurred in 1872, when a chemist was used to solve the infamous "torso murder" of Abijah Ellis. This nineteenth-century crime scene investigation involved the analysis of bloodstains on the accused man's clothes, which proved to be consistent with the blood of Ellis, whose body had been found floating in a barrel on the Charles River.

In an 1858 novel, Dr. Oliver Wendell Holmes Sr., dubbed the Massachusetts State House the "Hub of the Solar System." The nickname evolved over the years to encompass the whole of Boston, which came to be known as the "Hub of the Universe" and, eventually, "The Hub."

Visitors to Boston often wonder how to decode the flashing lights on the roof of the Old Hancock Building, which can be read using this helpful verse: "Solid blue, clear view/Flashing blue, clouds due/Solid red, rain ahead/Flashing red, snow ahead." The one exception to this rule is in summer, when flashing red means the Red Sox game is rained out.

"Boston Brahmin" is another term that owes its origins to Oliver Wendell Holmes, who memorably described the local elite as "The Brahmin Caste of New England." Though the word itself derives from the Indian caste system (in which Brahmins are regarded as members of the "highest or priestly caste among the Hindus"), it also relates to the American premiere of Brahms's Second Symphony, which was performed by the Boston Symphony at the Orpheum Theatre. Much of the audience walked out on the challenging piece of music, inspiring critics to call the ones who stayed "Brahmins."

Why "Beantown"? The nickname stems from the importance of beans in the economy of early Boston, but its sticking power is attributed to the city's surplus of molasses, which fostered the sweetened baked beans that came to be associated with Boston.

The first football game was played on Boston Common on November 7, 1863, organized by a team from Mr. Dixwell's private school on Boylston Street.

Partisans of obscure history should pay a special visit to the Omni Parker House, onetime site of the Saturday Club, a literary salon whose members included Ralph Waldo Emerson, Nathaniel Hawthorne, Henry Wadsworth Longfellow, and Oliver Wendell Holmes. Among the establishment's other claims to fame is the fact that Ho Chi Minh worked there (as a busboy), as did Malcolm X (as a waiter). John Wilkes Booth stayed there a week before he shot Abraham Lincoln, and John F. Kennedy announced his candidacy for Congress there in 1953.

Boston is home to the largest rowing meet in the world: the annual Head of the Charles Regatta, first held in 1965.

Though Boston is justifiably famous for the Big Dig excavation, much of the city owes its existence to early landfill projects. Neighborhoods reclaimed from the water include the Back Bay, the South End, and parts of South Boston.

Before the Red Sox won the World Series in 2004, superstitious fans went to great lengths to eliminate the so-called Curse of the Bambino (named for the fatefully traded Babe Ruth). Among the more extreme attempts to "reverse the curse" were placing a Red Sox cap at the summit of Mount Everest, then burning a Yankees cap at base camp; hiring exorcists to purify Fenway Park; and sending divers to recover a piano Ruth had pushed into a pond near his farm in Sudbury, Massachusetts.

America's first Catholic president, John F. Kennedy, was born in the Boston suburb of Brookline and assumed office in 1960. Forty-four years later, Boston's John Kerry became only the second Catholic to mount a major-party campaign for president, losing the election to the incumbent George W. Bush.

BIBLIOGRAPHY

Aronson, Marc. *Witch-Hunt: Mysteries of the Salem Witch Trials.* New York: Simon and Schuster, 2005.

Beatty, Jack. *The Rascal King: The Life and Times of James Michael Curley, 1874–1958.* Reading, Mass.: Addison-Wesley, 1992.

Behn, Noel. *Big Stick-Up at Brink's!* New York: Putnam, 1977.

Clark, Judith Freeman. *From Colony to Commonwealth: Massachusetts.* Northridge, Calif.: Windsor Publications, Inc., 1987.

Drake, Samuel Adams. *Old Landmarks and Historic Personages of Boston.* Rutland, Vt.: C. E. Tuttle, 1971.

Duncan, Russell. *Where Death and Glory Meet: Colonel Robert Gould Shaw and the Fifty-fourth Massachusetts Infantry.* Athens, Ga.: University of Georgia Press, 1999.

Fenster, Julie M. *Ether Day: The Strange Tale of America's Greatest Medical Discovery and the Haunted Men Who Made It.* New York: HarperCollins Publishers, 2001.

Feurlicht, Roberta Strauss. *Justice Crucified: The Story of Sacco and Vanzetti.* New York: McGraw-Hill, 1977.

Frank, Gerold. *The Boston Strangler.* New York: New American Library, 1966.

Freedman, Florence B. *Two Tickets to Freedom: The True Story of Ellen and William Craft, Fugitive Slaves.* New York: Scholastic Inc., 1971 (1993 printing).

Gitter, Elisabeth. *The Imprisoned Guest: Samuel Howe and Laura Bridgman, the Original Deaf-Blind Girl.* New York: Farrar, Straus and Giroux, 2001.

Jacobs, Donald, ed. *Courage and Conscience: Black and White Abolitionists in Boston.* Bloomington, Ind.: Published for the Boston Athenaeum by Indiana University Press, 1973.

King, Stephen, and Stewart O'Nan. *Faithful: Two Diehard Boston Red Sox Fans Chronicle the Historic 2004 Season.* New York: Scribner, 2004.

Lehr, Dick, and Gerard O'Neill. *Black Mass: The Irish Mob, the FBI, and a Devil's Deal.* New York: Public Affairs, 2000.

Lukas, J. Anthony. *Common Ground: A Turbulent Decade in the Lives of Three American Families.* Berkeley Heights, N.J.: Knopf (Distributed by Random House), 1985.

McCullough, David G. *1776.* New York: Simon and Schuster, 2005.

Miller, John Chester. *The Colonial Image: Origins of American Culture.* New York: G. Braziller, 1962.

Monroe, Judy. *The Sacco and Vanzetti Controversial Murder Trial: A Headline Court Case.* Berkeley Heights, N.J.: Enslow Publishers, 2000.

Puleo, Stephen. *Dark Tide: The Great Boston Molasses Flood of 1919.* Boston: Beacon Press, 2003.

Santella, Andrew. *The Boston Massacre*. New York: Children's Press, 2004.

Schorow, Stephanie. *Boston on Fire: A History of Fires and Firefighting in Boston*. Beverly, Mass.: Commonwealth Editions, 2003.

Schultz, Nancy Lusignan. *Fire and Roses: The Burning of the Charlestown Convent, 1834*. New York: Free Press, 2000.

Shaughnessy, Dan. *The Curse of the Bambino*. New York: Dutton, 1990.

―――. *Reversing the Curse: Inside the 2004 Boston Red Sox*. Boston: Houghton Mifflin, 2005.

Sherman, Casey. *A Rose for Mary: The Hunt for the Real Boston Strangler*. Boston: Northeastern University Press, 2003.

Snow, Edward Rowe. *Boston Bay Mysteries and Other Tales*. New York: Dodd, Mead, 1977.

Walker, David. *David Walker's Appeal, in Four Articles, Together with a Preamble, to the Coloured Citizens of the World, but in Particular, and Very Expressly, to Those in the United States of America*. Edited and with an introduction by Charles M. Wiltse. New York: Hill and Wang, 1965.

Zobel, Hiller B. *The Boston Massacre*. New York: W. W. Norton, 1970.

Zuckoff, Mitchell. *Ponzi's Scheme: The True Story of a Financial Legend*. New York: Random House, 2005.

Magazine and Newspaper Articles

Garrow, David J. "Toward a More Perfect Union." The *New York Times,* May 9, 2004.

Kuhr, Fred. "Boston's Legal Eagle: The Country's Most Powerful Lawyer in the Marriage Equality Fight Is Taking Her Case to Other States—and Trying to Avoid the Spotlight." *The Advocate,* January 18, 2005.

"Massachusetts Court Rules Ban on Gay Marriage Unconstitutional." *The Boston Globe,* February 4, 2004.

Other Media

Arce, Rose. "Massachusetts court upholds same-sex marriage." CNN. February 6, 2004. http://www.cnn.com/2004/LAW/02/04/gay.marriage.

Science of the Deep: The Wreck of the Portland. Television Documentary, The Science Channel, 2004.

Simon, Kirk, and Karen Goodman. *The American Experience: The Telephone.* Televised Film, PBS, 1997.

"Steamship Portland 2003." NOAA Ocean Explorer Web site: oceanexplorer.noaa.gov/explorations/03portland/welcome.html.

INDEX

ABOUT THE AUTHOR

Julia Boulton Clinger is a writer and editor whose first Boston address was a dog walk away from Old Ironsides and the Bunker Hill Monument. In addition to countless Freedom Trail expeditions with an aging basset hound and an infant son, she has written exhaustively about Boston for publications both local and national. A graduate of the Iowa Writer's Workshop and the Radcliffe Publishing Course, she earned her bachelor's and master's degrees from the University of Virginia.